Rocks, Gems, and Minerals

What You Need to Know about Crystals, Gemstones, Agates, and Other Rocks

© Copyright 2024 - All rights reserved.

The content contained within this book may not be reproduced, duplicated, or transmitted without direct written permission from the author or the publisher.

Under no circumstances will any blame or legal responsibility be held against the publisher, or author, for any damages, reparation, or monetary loss due to the information contained within this book, either directly or indirectly.

Legal Notice:

This book is copyright protected. It is only for personal use. You cannot amend, distribute, sell, use, quote, or paraphrase any part, or the content within this book, without the consent of the author or publisher.

Disclaimer Notice:

Please note the information contained within this document is for educational and entertainment purposes only. All effort has been executed to present accurate, up-to-date, reliable, and complete information. No warranties of any kind are declared or implied. Readers acknowledge that the author is not engaging in the rendering of legal, financial, medical, or professional advice. The content within this book has been derived from various sources. Please consult a licensed professional before attempting any techniques outlined in this book.

By reading this document, the reader agrees that under no circumstances is the author responsible for any losses, direct or indirect, that are incurred as a result of the use of the information contained within this document, including, but not limited to, errors, omissions, or inaccuracies.

Your Free Gift
(only available for a limited time)

Thanks for getting this book! If you want to learn more about various spirituality topics, then join Mari Silva's community and get a free guided meditation MP3 for awakening your third eye. This guided meditation mp3 is designed to open and strengthen ones third eye so you can experience a higher state of consciousness. Simply visit the link below the image to get started.

https://spiritualityspot.com/meditation

Table of Contents

INTRODUCTION 1
CHAPTER 1: THE BASICS OF ROCKS, GEMS, CRYSTALS, AND MINERALS 3
CHAPTER 2: IGNEOUS ROCKS 13
CHAPTER 3: SEDIMENTARY ROCKS 24
CHAPTER 4: METAMORPHIC ROCKS 38
CHAPTER 5: MINERALS AND CRYSTAL SYSTEMS 52
CHAPTER 6: QUARTZ 62
CHAPTER 7: CHALCEDONIES AND AGATES 75
CHAPTER 8: PRECIOUS GEMSTONES 84
CHAPTER 9: SEMI-PRECIOUS GEMSTONES 92
CHAPTER 10: METEORITES AND TEKTITES 100
APPENDIX: A-Z OF ROCKS, CRYSTALS, GEMS, AND MINERALS 107
CONCLUSION 109
HERE'S ANOTHER BOOK BY MARI SILVA THAT YOU MIGHT LIKE 111
YOUR FREE GIFT (ONLY AVAILABLE FOR A LIMITED TIME) 112
REFERENCES 113

Introduction

Do you have a passion for rocks and gems? Are you looking to build a collection or turn your interest into a business? This guide will cover all these topics and more.

Rocks, gems, and minerals may appear to be mundane objects to some, but they contain a wealth of knowledge about our planet. Taking a closer look at these earthly wonders reveals some incredible facts. For example, many types of gemstones are formed under extreme pressure and temperatures so intense that our bodies cannot survive them. They also exist in a dizzying variety of colors and shapes, each with its own unique composition. Uncovering more about rocks, gems, and minerals can provide an exciting window into the natural world around us. It's an opportunity for exploration that is sure to bring delight!

Rocks have the power to transport us back across time, as many as millions of years ago. Though inanimate, they nevertheless tell tales that span multiple eras. These geological stories can help us further understand our planet's history and present conditions. On the other side of the geological spectrum lie gems and minerals. While gems are prized for their beautiful shimmer - and what is deemed rare beauty - minerals are more valued for their practical use in construction projects. From walls to roads, minerals comprise the basic building blocks that allow larger structures to exist. It's incredible how one simple rock can tell a story that spans millennia, offers unconditional beauty, and can simultaneously be used in crucial engineering endeavors.

Learning about these wonders of nature helps us connect with our Earth's origins and appreciate them in our everyday lives. This guide will explore each type of rock and mineral, teaching you their individual characteristics and helping you identify them. This guide will show you how to use them in a variety of ways, from creating jewelry to collecting specimens. From ore to crystals, this guide will provide you with the essential knowledge you need to make the most of your rocks and gems.

This comprehensive guide is ready to take you on a journey through the fascinating world of rocks, gems, and minerals. By the end, you'll have the tools to become a rock and mineral expert like never before. The simple and easy-to-understand layout makes it a great resource for novice and experienced enthusiasts alike. So read on to discover what these fantastic objects can teach you!

Chapter 1: The Basics of Rocks, Gems, Crystals, and Minerals

Do you know what makes up the Earth's crust? When we look at a landscape or stepping stones leading to our front door, we look at rocks. When we admire a diamond or an opal, we look at gemstones. And when we hold a rose quartz crystal or a piece of pyrite, we look at minerals. Rocks, gems, and minerals each have characteristics that make them distinct.

This chapter explores the scientific definitions of rocks, gems, and minerals. It will discuss how they are formed and uncover the different types of each. It will also introduce some fun facts about them that you may have never heard before!

Rocks

Rocks are fascinating geological objects which help us understand our environment. They come in all shapes and sizes, from tiny stones to mammoth boulders, and each one offers a better glimpse into the world of science. Rocks are composed of minerals or pieces from previously existing rocks and are created naturally through geologic processes. Rocks form when sediment is compressed and heated by tectonic forces, allowing them to take on specific characteristics depending on their environment. Rocks play an integral role in our understanding of the universe around us.

The study of rocks gives us insight into many mysteries of our planet and how it was formed over the ages.

https://unsplash.com/photos/66BgmIglPhM

Rock Formations

Nothing beats a great adventure outdoors to appreciate rock formations' incredible beauty. Not only are they mesmerizing for their sheer size, but many areas have different types of rock formations that boast dazzling colors from crushed minerals and even fossils from other life forms. Exploring those smaller details can be especially rewarding when paired with spectacular views composed of ancient mountains eroded over time. The awe-inspiring grandeur of some unusual rock formations can make for an unforgettable experience.

Types of Rocks

From the Grand Canyon to Mount Everest and even the roads we drive on, rocks are the foundation of the Earth. The Earth's crust comprises millions of different kinds of rocks, but do you know that there are only three types? These three types have specific characteristics and are formed through different processes.

1. Igneous Rocks

Igneous rocks are the most commonly found on the Earth's surface. These rocks form when molten rock material, magma, cools and solidifies. Depending on where they form, igneous rocks can be categorized as extrusive or intrusive.

When magma cools and hardens gradually *beneath the earth's surface*, intrusive igneous rocks are created. On the other hand, extrusive igneous rocks are created *on the earth's surface* as magma rapidly solidifies and cools. Some examples of igneous rocks include basalt, granite, and pumice.

2. Sedimentary Rocks

Sedimentary rocks are formed when weathering and erosion break down rocks into small fragments that get transported to a new place by water or wind. These pieces –referred to as sediment – are deposited and compacted in the new place. Sedimentary rock is the end product. Clastic, chemical, and organic sedimentary rocks can be further divided into categories. The collection of grains and rock pieces results in clastic rocks. Shale and sandstone are two examples. Chemical rocks form from the precipitation of minerals from water. An example of this is limestone. Organic rocks, such as coal and fossils, are composed of the remains of plants and animals.

3. Metamorphic Rocks

Metamorphic rocks are formed when existing rocks get transformed by immense heat and pressure. They are often found at the site of mountain-building processes, where tectonic plates collide, creating high temperatures and pressures. Foliated and non-foliated metamorphic rocks can be distinguished based on the source rock. Due to the arrangement of minerals under intense pressure, foliated metamorphic rocks appear layered or banded. Slate and Gneisss are two examples. The surface of non-foliated metamorphic rocks is uniform and rough. Quartzite and marble are two examples.

Every rock on Earth falls into igneous, sedimentary, or metamorphic. The type of rock and its characteristics reveal valuable information about its history and the processes that occurred to create it. Understanding each rock type's properties is essential in geology, mining, and environmental conservation. So, the next time you come across rocks on your walks, remember these simple entities are more than just pebbles. They are a fundamental piece of the Earth's history.

Interesting Facts about Rocks

Rocks are one of the most fascinating subjects that everyone can appreciate. Even though they might not seem like much, they possess a range of interesting facts that people might not be aware of. From precious stones to ordinary gravel, rocks play an essential role in our daily lives. Here are some interesting facts about rocks that will surely spark your curiosity.

- The moon is made up of rocks called lunar rocks, and scientists have been studying them since 1969 when Apollo 11 landed on the moon.
- Did you know that the world's largest rock is in Australia? It's called Uluru, also known as Ayers Rock. This sandstone rock stands nearly 348 meters high and measures 9.4 kilometers in circumference.
- Did you know that some rocks can float? Pumice is a type of volcanic rock that is filled with gas bubbles. This unique structure makes it light enough to float on water.
- Did you know how old rocks can be? Some rocks, such as granite, can be as old as 3 billion years! Some of the rocks you see in your backyard could have formed within the very first days of Earth's history.
- Did you know that there is a special type of rock called Tektites? Tektites are formed when meteors impact the Earth's surface and melt the rocks around it. These melted rocks are then forced into the atmosphere and eventually fall back to Earth as Tektites.

Rocks hold a valuable history of the Earth's past, and studying their composition can provide essential clues about past geological activities. It's like a time capsule with secrets about the early Earth's environment, conditions, and the organisms that once roamed it.

Gems

Humans have always been fascinated with shiny, rare objects that can be worn as jewelry. And there's no object more precious than a gemstone. Gems are more than just objects of beauty. They are minerals formed deep beneath the Earth's surface that take millions of years to develop. The mysteries of their journey from the Earth's crust to our jewelry boxes are enchanting. Let's dive deeper into the world of precious stones to satisfy your curiosity.

Definition

In the simplest form, gems are rocks valued for their rarity, beauty, and durability. They are formed deep within the Earth's mantle, under extreme pressure and heat. Geological activities such as volcanic eruptions and earthquakes cause gems to rise to the Earth's surface, where they are discovered by humans. Though diamonds are the most sought-after gemstone, many other precious and semi-precious gems such as rubies, emeralds, sapphires, topaz, and more exist.

How They Are Formed

There are various ways in which gems can be formed, depending on the minerals that have been subjected to heat and intense pressure beneath the Earth's mantle. For example, diamonds are formed when carbon goes through extreme pressure and temperature, typically found deep within the Earth, up to 150 to 200 km deep. Alternatively, some gems may also be formed through geological processes like volcanic activity, erosion, or mining. These processes can take millions of years, which is why gems are considered rare and valuable.

Setting the Value

Apart from their formation, the beauty of the gemstones also depends on their color, cut, and clarity. While formed under high pressure, different minerals cause color variations, commonly called the "chroma." Some gems require specialized treatment to enhance their natural color and transparency, while others can be used in their raw form. The gem's cut refers to the proportions and symmetry of the facets or flat surfaces. Through cutting, gems are fashioned into different shapes, such as round, oval, or princess, multiplying their worth in turn.

Gemstones are easy to purchase, and their value largely depends on the "four Cs" carat, cut, color, and clarity. The carat refers to the weight of the stone, whereas color is an important aspect of higher-priced gems. Clarity is the lack of inclusions, the naturally occurring imperfections, and the cut refers to the facets' number, position, and angles.

Types of Gemstones

Gems have always been as charming as the mystery of their origin. They have been serving mankind as a sign of luxury and prosperity since time immemorial. Let's take a deeper look at different types of gemstones:

1. Precious Stones

The term "precious" indicates scarcity, high quality, and cost. The four precious stones are diamonds, rubies, emeralds, and sapphires. Diamond is the epitome of all precious stones. It is the hardest mineral on Earth, looks stunning in its colorless form, and its luster is enhanced if colored. Ruby is the iconic red gemstone that signifies love, courage, and protection. Emerald is a green gemstone that symbolizes beauty, elegance, and rebirth. Sapphire is a blue gemstone that represents sincerity, loyalty, and peace. Precious stones have been used in royal jewelry and engagement rings for centuries due to their rarity and durability.

2. Semi-Precious Stones

The term "semi-precious" indicates abundance, lower cost, and lower hardness. Semi-precious stones encompass a broad range of mineral specimens. Some popular examples are amethyst, garnet, peridot, topaz, and turquoise. Amethyst is a purple gemstone that represents wisdom, peace, and intuition. Garnet is a red gemstone that symbolizes protection, strength, and confidence. Peridot is a green gemstone that signifies healing, balance, and growth. Topaz is a yellow gemstone representing good fortune, success, and creativity. Turquoise is a blue-green gemstone that symbolizes friendship, communication, and protection. Semi-precious stones are an affordable choice for everyday jewelry and offer a diverse selection of colors and designs.

Main Differences

The main differences between precious and semi-precious stones are their costs, hardness, rarity, and symbolism. Precious stones are more expensive than semi-precious stones due to their scarcity, quality, and origin. Semi-precious stones are cheaper but still offer a vibrant range of colors and shapes. Precious gems have a higher score on the Mohs hardness scale, which means they are more resistant to scratches and damage. Semi-precious stones are softer and require more precautions to maintain their luster over time. Precious gemstones are rarer and have a more significant meaning in the world of jewelry because of their tradition and value. Semi-precious gemstones have more cultural diversity and offer a broader range of possible symbols and purposes.

Interesting Facts about Gemstones

There is no denying that gems are more than just jewelry. They are natural treasures with remarkable stories to tell. From their formation to their journey to our jewelry boxes, the precious stones have an awe-inspiring journey that makes them extremely valuable. Here are some interesting facts about gemstones:

- Did you know that more than 4,000 different mineral species exist on Earth?
- Opal is the only gemstone to display all of the rainbow's colors simultaneously.
- The world's oldest diamond is estimated to be 3.2 billion years old!
- Rubies are one of the few gems that can be found in the same color as they were when first mined.
- Emeralds are the rarest of all precious stones, and some can cost hundreds of thousands of dollars!
- Amethysts are believed to have healing and spiritual qualities.

The rarity, beauty, and durability of gems make them a perfect symbol of love and friendship and an ideal collection to pass down to the next generation. Don't underestimate the gemstones' allure and ability to transform your outfit and mood. As the saying goes, "Diamonds are forever," and so is the enduring beauty of all other gems. So, choose the gemstone that speaks to you, and cherish it for life.

Minerals

Regarding natural resources, minerals have always been a fascinating subject of study. Revered for their beauty, value, and industrial applications, minerals can be found on every continent and across every ocean. This section will take a closer look at the world of minerals, defining what they are, their properties, and how they're formed. Whether you're a collector, student, or simply curious about the subject, this information will enrich your understanding of the beauty and complexity of minerals.

Minerals occur naturally in our world and have a crystalline structure with a defined chemical composition. A substance must be naturally formed without human intervention and have a unique crystal structure to be considered a mineral. Some of the most common minerals include quartz, feldspar, calcite, and olivine. Each mineral is unique and can be distinguished by its structure, color, hardness, and other factors.

Mineral Properties

Minerals have a range of physical properties that distinguish them from one another. These properties include luster, cleavage, and hardness.

- **Luster:** the way minerals reflect light
- **Hardness:** the resistance of a mineral to scratching
- **Cleavage:** the way any mineral splits along clean planes

These properties can be used to identify a mineral, along with its color and other characteristics. Some minerals, like diamonds, are known for their extreme hardness, while others, like sulfur, are prized for their vivid colors.

Mineral Formations

Minerals are formed in various ways, often through the slow cooling and crystallization of magma or the mineral deposit left from evaporating bodies of water. In some cases, minerals grow over long periods in rock cavities, forming unique and intricate crystal structures. Other minerals, like gold and silver, are formed deep within the Earth and are mined for their value. Some minerals can even form through biological processes, such as the formation of shells and bones. Understanding the different ways in which minerals are formed can give us insight into the history and geology of the Earth.

Types of Minerals

Geologists classify minerals as inorganic, naturally occurring compounds with a particular chemical makeup and crystal structure. These rocks and minerals are vital in various facets of our daily lives, including technology, agriculture, construction, and medicine. Let's take a closer look at the different types of minerals and their uses and discover their role in our day-to-day activities.

1. Native Elements

Native elements are minerals that are composed of single elements. They are relatively rare, but some of them, such as gold (Au), copper (Cu), and silver (Ag), are very coveted for their beauty and value. Gold, for example, has been used for millennia as a form of currency, jewelry, and even dental fillings. On the other hand, copper is instrumental in conducting electricity and is used in various electronic devices like smartphones and laptops.

2. Silicates

The largest group of minerals is silicates which comprise nearly 90% of the Earth's crust. This group includes feldspar, mica, quartz, and clay. Silicates are useful in the production of ceramics, construction materials, and electronic components. For example, quartz is an essential component of watches and electronic components. The right balance of quartz ensures that they keep accurate time.

3. Oxides and Hydroxides

Oxides and hydroxides contain oxygen and hydrogen atoms but different numbers of cations. Hematite is one of the most common oxides and is used in pigments, jewelry, and the production of iron. Bauxite, another oxide, is used in the production of aluminum. Hydroxides, on the other hand, are important components of soil chemistry and are used in wastewater treatment plants.

4. Sulfates and Carbonates

Sulfates and carbonates are minerals that play a significant role in construction, agriculture, and medicine. Sulfates are components of gypsum and are used in the production of wallboard, cement, and fertilizer. Carbonates include minerals like calcite, dolomite, and aragonite – essential components of limestone and marble. They are used in the production of cement and other construction materials.

5. Halides

Halides are minerals that contain halogen atoms, such as chlorine, fluorine, bromine, or iodine. Fluorite, for example, is used in producing hydrofluoric acid, which is used in the semiconductor industry. Halides are also used as salt in various food products, while iodine is used in producing X-ray contrast agents and iodized salt.

These five major groups of minerals are just a few of the many types found within the Earth's crust. Each type's unique properties and characteristics make them invaluable in various industries and applications. As science advances, we are sure to uncover more uses for rocks and minerals.

Interesting Facts about Minerals

While it may seem like minerals are just rocks and stones, they have a variety of properties that make them truly fascinating. Here are some interesting facts about minerals:

- The world's oldest known mineral is zircon, which was discovered in rocks dating back over 4 billion years old!
- The diamond is the hardest mineral, with a hardness of 10 on the Mohs scale.
- Some minerals are fluorescent, meaning they glow when exposed to certain types of light.
- Aquamarine, the official birthstone for March, is a blue-green variety of beryl.
- "Mineral" comes from the Latin word for "to lead," referring to the idea that minerals could be melted and molded into shapes.
- Some minerals, such as opal, contain water trapped in their structure.
- Calcite is the most common sedimentary mineral and is formed by the precipitation of calcium carbonate from water.
- The largest crystal ever found was a giant selenite weighing 55 tons and measuring 11 meters long!

Exploring the world of minerals can be a fascinating and enriching experience. From their definition to their unique properties and formations, minerals offer a glimpse into the natural world and the complexity of the Earth. Whether you're a passionate collector or simply interested in learning more, understanding the world of minerals can help us appreciate the natural world in new and exciting ways.

Rocks, gems, and minerals are integral to the Earth's makeup and essential materials for our daily lives. Rocks are aggregates of minerals that form when minerals cool and solidify. Gemstones are minerals cut and polished to create beautiful jewelry pieces. By understanding the different types available in nature, we can appreciate their integral role in our day-to-day lives. These natural wonders remain essential to the modern world, from simple construction materials to precious gems.

Chapter 2: Igneous Rocks

Have you ever been amazed by the natural beauty around you? From stunning landscapes to intriguing rock formations, the natural world has its way of leaving us in awe. Igneous rocks are a fascinating aspect of the natural world that hold valuable information about the Earth's history. From the slow-cooling granite to the rapid-cooling obsidian, each igneous rock has a particular story to tell. The significance of igneous rocks lies in their place in geology.

This chapter will explore the nature of igneous rocks, their formation process, and how to identify them. Firstly, the four categories of igneous rocks (felsic, intermediate, mafic, and ultramafic) will be examined, and examples of each type will be provided. Finally, some tips for identifying these types of rocks in their natural environment will be discussed. By the end, you'll better understand them and their significance in geology.

Overview of Igneous Rocks

One of the most awe-inspiring sights in nature is a volcano erupting. The lava flows, the pyroclastic explosions, and the fiery flares of molten rock are a spectacle to behold. But have you ever wondered what happens to all that magma once it has cooled and hardened? The answer is igneous rocks. The world of igneous rocks is fascinating, from their formation to their different types and unique features.

What Are Igneous Rocks?

Igneous rocks are formed from solidified magma or lava that has cooled and crystallized. The word igneous comes from the Latin word *ignis*, meaning fire. These rocks are created underground or above the Earth's surface during volcanic activity. Igneous rocks are among the most common types of rocks on the planet, and they can be found in various locations, from volcanic islands to mountain ranges and even in the depths of the ocean.

How Are Igneous Rocks Formed?

As mentioned before, igneous rocks are formed by solidifying molten rock material, whether above or below the Earth's surface. Intrusive or plutonic igneous rocks include granite, while an example of extrusive or volcanic igneous rocks includes basalt. Volcanic eruptions can also cause pyroclastic flows, forming tuff, ash, and other igneous rocks.

Types of Igneous Rocks

Igneous rocks can be classified into two major categories, intrusive and extrusive. Extrusive igneous rocks have a fine-grained texture due to their rapid cooling and lack of visible crystals, like obsidian or basalt. Intrusive igneous rocks are characterized by visible crystals on their surface and have a coarse-grained texture, like granite or diorite.

Igneous rocks can also be classified based on their mineral composition. Mafic (or basaltic) rocks are high in iron and magnesium and have a dark color. On the other hand, Felsic (or granitic) rocks are high in silicon and aluminum and are usually lighter in color. Intermediate rocks have a mineral composition in between mafic and felsic rocks. These rocks are fascinating and beautiful natural formations. Their unique features and formation process make them essential in our understanding of Earth's geology. The next time you come across a rocky outcrop or a volcanic landscape, you'll be able to identify the type of rock formation and appreciate the beauty and wonder of igneous rocks.

Felsic Rocks

When it comes to understanding the Earth's crust, rocks are a crucial component that tells us a lot about the geological history of our planet. The Earth's crust comprises different types of rocks, including igneous rocks. Felsic rocks are one of these fascinating igneous rocks with very particular compositions and characteristics. The term felsic comes from the words feldspar and silica, which are two of its primary components.

Examples of Felsic Rocks

Felsic rocks are light in color and rich in silicon, aluminum, potassium, calcium, sodium, and oxygen. Some of the most common types of felsic rocks include granite, rhyolite, and pumice. Granite is a coarse-grained rock and the most prevalent type of felsic rock. On the other hand, Rhyolite is a fine-grained volcanic rock, rich in silicon, making it resistant to weathering. Pumice is a type of volcanic rock that floats in water, and it appears in different shapes, including volcanic glass with bubbles.

Granite is an example of a popular felsic rock.
James St. John, CC BY 2.0 <https://creativecommons.org/licenses/by/2.0>, via Wikimedia Commons https://commons.wikimedia.org/wiki/File:Granite_26_(49199871943).jpg

Characteristics of Felsic Rocks

One of the critical features of felsic rocks is their composition, which consists of high levels of silica and alkali metal oxides such as potassium and sodium. These minerals give felsic rocks their light color and resistance to weathering. Felsic rocks also have a higher viscosity than mafic rocks, which implies that they resist flowing as quickly as mafic rocks. Besides, felsic rocks often have visible crystals, which give them a distinctive appearance. This type of rock is also associated with explosive volcanic eruptions.

Tips to Find Felsic Rocks

If you're trying to find felsic rocks, one of the best places to start is in mountain ranges, particularly in regions with a lot of volcanic activity. Another way to find felsic rocks is to search for exposed rocks with visible crystals. Granite, for example, is an excellent place to find felsic rocks since the visible crystals can be seen with the naked eye. Finally, you can look for areas of the landscape with different colored rocks, particularly those with red or pink tones.

Uses of Felsic Rocks

Felsic rocks, or igneous rocks rich in the elements of feldspar and quartz, are fascinating creations of the natural world and have many uses. From roofing tiles to applications in geothermal energy, these versatile rocks have been a boon to humanity and industry. Felsic rocks can also act as aquifers for water storage, and their formations often include valuable minerals like quartz and gold. They have even been used to fill lake and ocean beds for land reclamation. Felsic rocks can also be seen in some of the most stunning landscapes on Earth. From towering ash clouds billowing at volcanoes to glimmering lava flows coating hillsides, they truly do make up some of nature's most beautiful artwork.

These rocks are a fascinating component of the Earth's crust. Their composition and characteristics make them easily distinguishable from other types of igneous rocks. From their rich colors to their unique mineral makeup, felsic rocks are a fascinating topic for both geologists and rock enthusiasts. These rocks were formed by magma that was rich in silica, resulting in a distinctive texture and appearance. Looking closely, you may even spot some feldspar or quartz minerals embedded within the rock. Felsic rocks are a testament to the intricate and complex nature of our planet's geology, a reminder of the fascinating forces that continue to shape our world today.

Intermediate Rocks

Are you passionate about rock collecting and want to take your hobby to the next level? Intermediate rocks could be a fascinating new challenge for you. These rocks are more complex than basic rocks yet less intense than advanced-level rocks. Intermediate rocks offer a variety of unique colors and patterns that will keep you engaged for hours. This section will discuss the characteristics and examples of intermediate rocks and provide you with some tips on how to find them.

Examples of Intermediate Rocks

Intermediate rocks are mainly classified based on their chemical composition. These rocks have a silica content ranging from 52% to 66%. Some popular examples of intermediate rocks are andesite, diorite, and trachyte.

Andesite is an example of an intermediate rock.
Smithsonian Institution, CC0, via Wikimedia Commons
https://commons.wikimedia.org/wiki/File:Basaltic_Andesite_from_Paricutin_volcano_in_Mexico_-_Smithsonian_Rock_Sample.jpg

- **Andesite** rocks have a medium-gray color tone and are usually identified by their fine-grained structure. You will often find black, white, or brown mineral deposits in andesite rocks.
- **Diorite** is a coarse-grained rock with a salt and pepper-like appearance that comes from the mingling of dark and light minerals. Mica and amphibole minerals are to be found in this rock type.
- **Trachyte** rocks are often identified by their dull gray color and fine-grained structure. These rocks are composed of alkali feldspar, plagioclase feldspar, and small amounts of biotite, hornblende, and other minerals.

Characteristics of Intermediate Rocks

Intermediate rocks are distinguished by their unique features. They are often dark gray or light green, with spots or streaks of black, white, or brown minerals. The grains within these rocks are neither too fine nor too large and can be seen with the naked eye. Intermediate rocks are also denser than basic rocks, which makes them harder and more resistant to erosion. These rocks often have a more complex internal structure with layers and bands of different minerals. The mineral composition determines its strength, durability, and resistance. These rocks often contain a mix of feldspar, quartz, and mica minerals.

Tips to Find Intermediate Rocks

Intermediate rocks can be found in a variety of locations. If you are looking for diorite, search for outcrops around granite, volcanic rocks, or mountain-building zones. Andesite rocks can often be found in areas with recent volcanic activity or the areas of the Pacific Basin. Trachyte rocks are found in locations that were once sea floors but now make up dry land. Look for exposed rocky outcrops with white, gray, or pale green shades around these areas. When searching for intermediate rocks, keep an eye out for the distinctive patterns and textures that characterize these rocks. Try to look for rocks along riverbeds, streams, or dry lakebeds. You could also check where rocks have been recently exposed within road cuts or construction sites.

Uses of Intermediate Rocks

From forming the foundation of roads and sidewalks to providing a protective barrier around buildings, intermediate rocks are essential for residential and commercial projects. They also play a key role in creating bridges and large-scale structures, making it possible to build spans that can support a tremendous amount of weight. Quite impressive, don't you think? The uses of intermediate rocks extend far beyond these practical purposes as well. They have been featured in architectural works of art such as sculptures and monuments, adding structural stability without compromising aesthetics. From utilitarian to stylish, intermediate rocks always deliver remarkable results!

Rock collecting can be an enriching and fascinating hobby. With intermediate rocks, you can explore an even more complex area of rock collecting, discover unusual colors and patterns, and grow your knowledge about these interesting rocks.

Mafic Rocks

Have you ever heard of mafic rocks? Well, if you haven't, then you're in for a treat because we're going to explore the wonders of these amazing rocks. Mafic rocks are some of the most common in the world and can be found almost everywhere. They may not be as well-known as their cousin, granite, but they are just as important. So, let's dive into the world of mafic rocks and learn all about their examples, characteristics, and tips to find them.

Examples of Mafic Rocks

Mafic rocks are also known as basaltic rocks, and one of the best-known is basalt. Basalt is a volcanic rock often found near the surface of the Earth. It is usually a dark color with a fine-grained texture, known for its durability and resistance to weathering. Another example of a mafic rock is gabbro, an intrusive rock usually found deeper in the Earth's crust. It is often used as a construction material due to its strength and durability.

Gabbro is an example of a mafic rock.
James St. John, CC BY 2.0 DEED
<https://creativecommons.org/licenses/by/2.0/>https://www.flickr.com/photos/jsjgeology/49943337113

Characteristics of Mafic Rocks

Mafic rocks are characterized by their high levels of magnesium and iron. They are high in density, dark in color, and have a low silica content. Mafic rocks are also known for their ability to conduct heat and electricity, making them useful in various industrial applications. They can be formed below and above the Earth's surface and come in a range of textures, from fine-grained to coarse-grained.

Tips to Find Mafic Rocks

Mafic rocks can be found in various environments, including volcanic regions, oceanic crust, and even some mountain ranges. One of the best ways to find them is to look for areas with volcanic activity. The lava flows that come from volcanoes are often made up of mafic rocks like basalt. Another way to find mafic rocks is to look for areas of exposed bedrock, especially where erosion occurs. Look for dark-colored rocks with a coarse texture; these are often signs of mafic rocks.

Uses of Mafic Rocks

Mafic rocks have many uses, including construction, roadwork, and industrial applications. Basalt, for example, is often used as a building material for both residential and commercial structures. It is also used in constructing roads and bridges due to its durability and strength. Gabbro is used in countertops, flooring, gravestones, and markers due to its resistance to wear and tear. Mafic rocks are also used in steel production, as they can be added to the molten metal to increase its strength.

Mafic rocks may not have the same popularity as their cousin, granite, but they are just as crucial. The high levels of magnesium and iron in mafic rocks make them useful in various applications, from construction to industrial uses. So, the next time you come across a dark, dense rock, take a closer look, and you might be looking at a magnificent mafic rock.

Ultramafic Rocks

Nature is full of surprises, and exploring rocks and minerals is one of the best ways to discover what our planet offers. Ultramafic rocks are a particular type of rock that is fascinating to study due to their unique characteristics. If you love geology and are curious about ultramafic rocks, then read on and learn all about these incredible rocks.

Examples of Ultramafic Rocks

Ultramafic rocks are a group of igneous and metamorphic rocks which are composed predominantly of minerals with a high magnesium and iron content. Some common examples of ultramafic rocks are peridotite, dunite, pyroxenite, and serpentinite. Peridotite is the most abundant type of ultramafic rock and is commonly found in the Earth's mantle. Dunite is a type of peridotite that is almost entirely made up of olivine. Pyroxenite is composed mainly of pyroxene minerals like augite and enstatite, while serpentinite is formed by the alteration of ultramafic rocks under the influence of water.

Peridotite is an example of ultramafic rocks.
James St. John, CC BY 2.0 <https://creativecommons.org/licenses/by/2.0>, via Wikimedia Commons https://commons.wikimedia.org/wiki/File:Peridotite_mantle_xenoliths_in_vesicular_phonotephrite_(Peridot_Mesa_Flow,_Middle_Pleistocene,_580_ka;_Peridot_Mesa,_San_Carlos_Volcanic_Field,_Arizona)_7_(1499 2925414).jpg

Characteristics of Ultramafic Rocks

Ultramafic rocks have several characteristics which distinguish them from other rock types. Firstly, they are rich in magnesium and iron, which give them a characteristic dark green to black color. They also have a high density, making them heavier than most other types of rock. Ultramafic rocks are also known for their resistance to weathering, erosion, and chemical breakdown, due to the high stability of their mineral content. This is why they are often found as exposed outcrops and are sometimes used in construction as durable building materials.

Tips to Find Ultramafic Rocks

One of the best ways to find ultramafic rocks is to look for them in areas with geologically active tectonic processes. Specifically, areas with mantle upwellings or areas of past geological activity like ophiolite complexes can be ideal locations for finding ultramafic rocks. These rocks are usually closer to the Earth's surface along fault lines and fractures, so searching for areas where rocks are exposed or accessible can be helpful. Ultramafic rocks are also valuable sources of minerals like chromite and nickel, making them of interest to mining companies. Thus, taking a mining tour can also provide an opportunity to see ultramafic rocks up close.

Uses of Ultramafic Rocks

Ultramafic rocks are rich in raw materials and can be used for various purposes. They make up the thickest section of the Earth's mantle and hold valuable iron, magnesium, chromium, gold, and platinum deposits. Ultramafic rocks are ideal for manufacturing essential items like cellular phones and television sets because they contain both ferromagnesian silicate minerals with large amounts of magnesium and iron.

Ultramafic rocks are also an excellent source of refractory metals such as titanium, tungsten, chromium, molybdenum, cobalt, and beryllium, which help protect sensitive equipment when exposed to extreme temperatures or conditions. In addition to their industrial uses, ultramafic rocks play a significant role in environmental science because they contain minerals that absorb pollutants from runoff water or forest fires. Truly invaluable natural resources!

Ultramafic rocks are fascinating geological marvels worth exploring if you are interested in geology. With their unique characteristics, they provide a glimpse into the inner workings of our planet and offer insights into how our world came to be. By taking some time to study and explore them, you can gain a better understanding and appreciation of the natural world around us.

Identifying Igneous Rocks

With their interesting textures and vibrant colors, igneous rocks are truly a sight to behold. From silky smooth obsidian to grainy granite, each igneous rock is a product of its own unique formation process. While identifying these rocks may seem daunting at first, once you start to notice the subtle differences in texture and appearance, you'll begin to understand the fascinating stories they have to reveal. Here are some tips to help you identify and classify igneous rocks.

- **Mineral Content:** Igneous rocks are made up of different minerals, each type having its own distinct mineral compositions. For example, felsic rocks typically comprise quartz, feldspar, mica, and other silicate components. Mafic rocks, on the other hand, contain more dark minerals such as olivine and pyroxene.

- **Texture:** Igneous rocks come in various textures, from smooth and glossy to coarse and grainy. Obsidian is an example of smooth and glossy igneous rock, while granite has a coarse, grainy texture.

- **Color:** Igneous rocks come in a variety of colors, from dark gray to yellow and pink. Pay attention to the overall hue of the rock and any variations in the color.
- **Visible Crystalline Structures:** Most igneous rocks contain at least some large crystalline structures that can be seen with the naked eye. Observe any patterns or shapes in these crystals to help identify the type of rock.

When it comes to identifying igneous rocks, practice makes perfect. The more you handle and observe these rocks, the more familiar you will become with their unique properties and characteristics. Additionally, don't be afraid to seek resources such as books, online guides, or fellow rock enthusiasts who can help you.

Igneous rocks are classified into extrusive or volcanic and intrusive or plutonic. Extrusive rocks cool down quickly on or near the Earth's surface, while intrusive rocks cool down slowly deep in the Earth's crust. Igneous rocks are also classified based on their mineral composition and texture and can range widely from fine-grained basalt to coarse-grained granite.

In conclusion, igneous rocks are an essential part of the Earth's geology, and understanding their properties and characteristics is crucial in fields such as geology, mining, and construction. While this chapter has only scratched the surface of what we know about igneous rocks, hopefully, it has sparked your interest and curiosity about the natural world. Geology is an exciting and ever-evolving field, so keep exploring and discovering, and who knows what amazing things you might find.

Chapter 3: Sedimentary Rocks

Have you ever wondered about the rocks which make up our planet's land surface? It may surprise you that most of these are called sedimentary rocks. From sandstone to shale and limestone, sedimentary rocks have been around for millions of years. They're more than just stunning geological formations. They also contain vital clues about the geologic history of our planet. Studying these remarkable rocks can open your eyes to untold stories of our Earth's evolution.

This chapter will explain the basics of sedimentary rocks, including their composition and characteristics. Also discussed will be the three categories of sedimentary rocks, clastic, organic, and chemical. After learning about these categories, specific types of sedimentary rocks, such as limestone, sandstone, siltstone, and shale, will be discussed. This chapter will end with a summary and the benefits of knowing about sedimentary rocks.

Introduction to Sedimentary Rocks

Sedimentary rocks are often taken for granted, mostly because they appear so common and plain and are seen everywhere. However, these rocks are not only abundant, but they also hold an extensive record of Earth's history. This is what makes sedimentary rocks fascinating to study. Let's uncover the stunning splendor that resides within sedimentary rocks as we delve deeper into their captivating world.

Formation of Sedimentary Rocks

Sedimentary rocks form when tiny particles and organic matter gather and amalgamate. These materials are then compressed and cemented together to form a solid rock. There are three main sedimentary rock types: clastic, chemical, and organic. Clastic sedimentary rocks are made when small pieces of rocks and minerals combine together. Chemical sedimentary rocks are formed from the precipitation of minerals from a solution. Organic sedimentary rocks are formed from the accumulation of shells, bones, and plant remains.

Layers and Formation

Sedimentary rocks are formed in layers, and each layer tells us a story about the past. Each layer's thickness, composition, and color give us clues about how the rock was formed and how the environment changed over time. The oldest layer is found at the bottom, while the most recent layer is at the top. The layers also reveal how the landscape has changed, including the presence of rivers, oceans, and deserts during different periods. We can learn about the history of climate, geography, and life on Earth through sedimentary rocks.

Common Sedimentary Rocks

Sandstone, limestone, and shale are some of the most common sedimentary rocks. Each of these rocks has unique properties and uses. Sandstone is made of sand grains cemented into solid rock. It is often used as a building material. Limestone is made of calcium carbonate, often deposited by shells and the remains of marine organisms. It is a popular building material and is also used in agriculture and industry. Shale is made of clay and often contains fossils. It is used as a source of oil and natural gas.

Uses of Sedimentary Rocks

Sedimentary rocks have a wide range of uses. They are used as building materials, such as sandstone, limestone, and slate. They are also used in agriculture. For example, limestone is used to raise the pH of acidic soils. Sedimentary rocks are also used in industry. For example, shale rock is used as a source of oil and natural gas. Furthermore, these rocks also have great value in geology as they provide insights into the history of our planet and how it has changed over time.

Clastic Sedimentary Rocks

Have you ever wondered how the Rocky Mountains and other canyons were formed? Or how volcanoes produce their distinctive rocks? Well, the answer probably lies in the world of sedimentary rocks. Of the three main types of rocks, sedimentary rocks make up most of the Earth's crust. Among the sub-classifications of sedimentary rocks are clastic rocks. Understanding clastic rocks can give you an understanding of the history of the Earth and how it evolved over millions of years.

Formation of Clastic Rocks

Clastic rocks are formed from the accumulation of rock or mineral particles or other small fragments, such as shells or fossils, that are transported and then deposited by water, ice, or wind. The name *clastic* comes from the Greek word *klastos*, which means "broken." There are numerous types of clastic rocks depending on their composition and the size of the particles. One common example is sandstone, formed by the accumulation of sand-sized grains cemented together. Shale, siltstone, and conglomerate rocks are other examples of clastic rocks that form through the compaction and cementation of sedimentary grains or clasts.

Siltstone.
James St. John, CC BY 2.0 DEED <https://creativecommons.org/licenses/by/2.0/>
https://www.flickr.com/photos/jsjgeology/36690094351

Characteristics of Clastic Rocks

This type of rock shares some common characteristics, like layers or bedding, which develop due to the sedimentation process. They are also porous and permeable, meaning they can hold and transmit fluids. Their color can vary from light to dark depending on their origin and composition. Clastic rocks can be hard or soft, depending on the degree of cementation, and they can be weathered or eroded easily. Some clastic rocks contain fossils, which provide clues about the past environment, climate, and formation of the rock.

Tips for Identifying Clastic Rocks

Identifying clastic rocks can be challenging, but with a few tips, you can start differentiating them from other types. One of the most noticeable features is the presence of different grain sizes or textures, which can be seen with the naked eye or with a magnifying glass. Another clue is their density and weight. Clastic rocks tend to be lighter compared to other rocks like igneous or metamorphic rocks. You can also test their hardness by scratching their surface with a knife or a nail. If the surface is easily scratched, it's probably a softer clastic rock like shale.

Understanding the world of clastic sedimentary rocks can provide a wealth of knowledge about the Earth's geology and history. By knowing their characteristics and identifying features, you can start to recognize them in different geological settings. Clastic rocks provide a window into the geological past, from the sandstone formations in Utah's national parks to the shale layers exposed in the Grand Canyon walls. So next time you take a hike or visit a natural wonder, remember to look for clues in the rocks around you and discover the amazing world of clastic sedimentary rocks.

Organic Sedimentary Rocks

Sedimentary rocks are truly amazing creations formed over millions of years under different geological conditions. One of the categories of this type of rock is organic sedimentary rock, which is formed through the accumulation of organic remains. These rocks are full of beauty and intrigue, and this section will explore the different types of organic sedimentary rocks, their characteristics, and how to identify them.

Examples of Organic Rocks

Organic sedimentary rocks are formed from the accumulation of organic matter, including coal, limestone, and chert. Coal is formed from the remains of ancient vegetation subjected to pressure and heat over millions of years. Limestone is formed from the accumulation of small shells and skeletons of marine organisms in seawater. Chert is formed from the accumulation of the hard remains of ancient sponges and sea squirts.

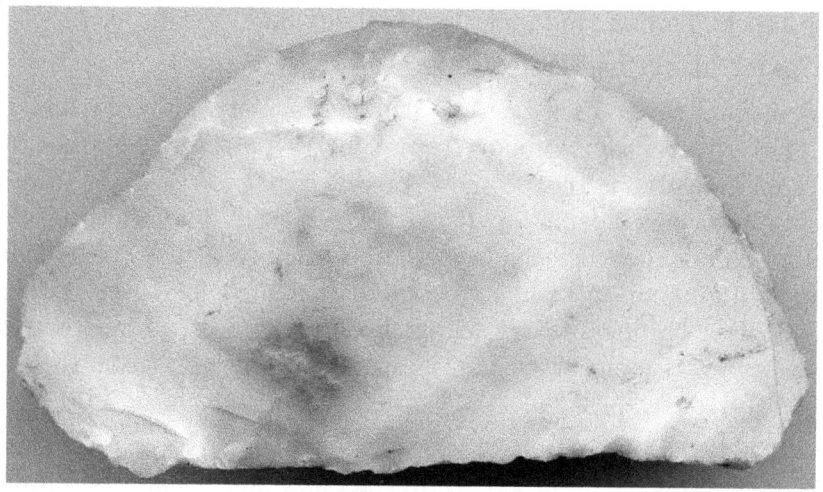

Chert.
James St. John, CC BY 2.0 DEED <https://creativecommons.org/licenses/by/2.0/>
https://www.flickr.com/photos/jsjgeology/16638766949

Characteristics of Organic Rocks

Organic sedimentary rocks exhibit characteristics that distinguish them from other sedimentary rocks. They are composed of organic matter, which gives them a dark color and an earthy odor. They also contain fossils and other organic remains often visible to the naked eye. When analyzed under a microscope, organic rocks have a granular or crystalline texture due to their organic composition.

Tips for Identifying Organic Rocks

The identification of organic rocks requires some knowledge of geology and paleontology. To identify an organic rock, it is crucial to examine its color, texture, and odor. Organic rocks are usually dark in color and have a distinctive earthy odor due to their organic composition. Their texture can be granular, crystalline, or nodular, depending on the type of organic matter that has been accumulated. You can also identify organic rocks by looking for fossils or other organic remains, such as shells or skeletons.

Another helpful tip is to examine the environment in which the rock was found. For example, limestone is often found near the ocean, while coal is found in land areas where ancient vegetation used to grow. This can provide clues as to the type of organic rock that you are dealing with.

Sedimentary organic rocks are a fascinating category of rocks that tells a story about the ancient environment in which they were formed. The accumulation of organic matter over millions of years can create a beautiful and unique rock full of surprises. By examining their color, texture, and environment of origin, you can identify and appreciate the beauty of organic rocks.

Chemical Sedimentary Rocks

Have you ever taken a stroll down a beach or along a rocky shoreline and noticed how varied the rock formations can be? No two rock formations are ever the same. Some are soft and crumbly, while others are hard and unyielding. Some are formed from layers of sand and silt, while others have been shaped by the sheer force of nature, like wind and water. But did you know some rocks are formed by chemical reactions right beneath our feet? Chemical sedimentary rocks may not be as glamorous as their igneous and metamorphic counterparts, but they are no less fascinating!

Examples of Chemical Rocks

Some common types of chemical sedimentary rocks include limestone, dolomite, rock salt, and chert. Limestone is probably the most commonly known and used. It is mainly made up of calcite, a mineral composed of calcium carbonate. Dolomite is similar to limestone but has a higher magnesium content. Rock salt, as the name implies, is composed mainly of halite, a mineral that forms from the evaporation of seawater. On the other hand, Chert is a hard, dense rock that forms from the accumulation of microscopic fossils and shells.

Dolomite.
Didier Descouens, CC BY-SA 4.0 <https://creativecommons.org/licenses/by-sa/4.0>, via Wikimedia Commons https://commons.wikimedia.org/wiki/File:Dolomite_Luzenac.jpg

Characteristics of Chemical Rocks

So, what sets chemical sedimentary rocks apart from other types of rocks? For one, they're formed by chemical processes rather than by erosion or melting. This means that they're usually formed in places like shallow lakes or oceans with high concentrations of dissolved minerals. They are also usually crystalline, meaning that they have a distinct structure and composition. Finally, chemical rocks are often characterized by layers or bands of different colors and textures, reflecting the varying conditions under which they were formed.

Tips for Identifying Chemical Rocks

If you're curious about these rocks and want to know how to identify them, there are a few things to look for. For starters, chemical rocks are usually quite hard and dense, with a crystalline or granular appearance. They are also often composed of relatively easy-to-recognize minerals like calcite, halite, or gypsum. Additionally, chemical rocks often have distinct layers or bands that reflect changes in the chemical makeup or environmental conditions from one period to another.

Chemical sedimentary rocks are an often overlooked but fascinating part of the geological landscape. From the sparkling crystals of halite to the dense layers of chert, these rocks represent the complex interplay of chemical and environmental factors that shape our world. Whether you're a professional geologist or just an amateur rock enthusiast, exploring and understanding these unique formations can help deepen your appreciation for the natural world around us!

Limestone

Limestone is an extremely popular sedimentary rock for its versatility, beauty, and durability. It has been used for various purposes for thousands of years and is still extensively used to this day. From construction to ornamental pieces, limestone is a hugely important natural resource.

Definition of Limestone

Limestone is formed from the mineral calcium carbonate. It comprises shells, coral, and other marine debris that have settled on the ocean floor and have been compacted and cemented over time. Limestone can vary in color and texture, from white to gray to tan, and may have different patterns and markings depending on the minerals present in the sediment that make up the rock.

Structure of Limestone

Limestone has a unique structure characterized by its porosity and permeability. It is a soft rock that can easily be carved and shaped but is also durable enough to withstand weathering and erosion. Limestone can comprise various layers or beds, which may have different compositions, thicknesses, and orientations. Some limestone deposits may contain fossils, which can provide valuable insights into the history of life and the environment.

Limestone.
Manishwiki15, CC BY-SA 3.0 <https://creativecommons.org/licenses/by-sa/3.0>, via Wikimedia Commons https://commons.wikimedia.org/wiki/File:Fossiliferous_Limestone.JPG

Uses of Limestone

Limestone has been used for a wide range of purposes, from construction to agriculture to art. It is a popular material for building and landscaping, as it is easy to work with, can be polished or textured, and has a classic, elegant look. Limestone is also used for making cement, as it contains high levels of calcium and magnesium. Additionally, limestone is a common ingredient in fertilizer, as it is rich in essential plant nutrients.

Tips for Identifying Limestone

If you are interested in identifying limestone, there are several things to look for. First, limestone is typically light in color, although it can come in various shades. It may be white, gray, or tan and have natural markings and patterns unique to each deposit. Limestone is also somewhat soft and can be scratched with a knife or nail. Finally, limestone is often found in areas that were once covered by shallow seas, such as beaches, cliffs, or quarries.

Limestone is an intriguing and versatile rock that has been used for centuries for a variety of purposes. Its unique structure and characteristics make it a popular resource for construction, agriculture, art, and more. Whether you are a geology enthusiast, a builder, a sculptor, or just curious about the world around you, learning about limestone can be a valuable and rewarding experience. With these tips for identifying limestone, you can explore the wonders of this beautiful rock and discover its many uses and applications.

Sandstone

When it comes to rocks and minerals, sandstone stands out for its beautiful colors, textures, and durability. This sedimentary rock has been used for centuries in construction, art, and various practical purposes. To better understand sandstone, let's explore its distinct structure, several of its various uses, and tricks to recognize it.

Definition of Sandstone

Sandstone is a type of rock comprising small grains of sand and minerals like feldspar or quartz. The grains are compacted and cemented together, forming a solid and hard rock. Sandstone is found in various colors, ranging from light beige and yellow to darker browns, reds, and even green.

Sandstone.
https://commons.wikimedia.org/wiki/File:Sandstone(quartz)USGOV.jpg

Structure of Sandstone

Sandstone has a unique structure which makes it different from other sedimentary rocks. It comprises small grains of sand visible to the naked eye. These grains vary in size and can be angular, rounded, or even partially melted due to extreme heat and pressure. The cement that binds these grains together can comprise silica, carbonate, or clay minerals. Some sandstones have layering or bedding planes, which are visible lines that separate the different layers formed over time.

Uses of Sandstone

Sandstone has been used for centuries in construction due to its durability and attractive appearance. Many historical buildings and monuments, such as The Taj Mahal, Petra, and The Grand Canyon, are made of sandstone. It is also used as a decorative stone, as it can be carved and sculpted into various shapes and designs. Sandstone is used in landscaping and garden design due to its natural and rustic look. It is also used as a material for paving, wall cladding, and flooring.

Tips for Identifying Sandstone

One of the best ways to identify sandstone is by its texture. Sandstone has a rough, grainy surface due to the visible grains of sand. Due to its density, it is also heavier than other rocks of the same size. You can also identify sandstone by its appearance. It has a visibly layered texture, and many sandstones have a rusty appearance due to the iron content in the minerals. Finally, you can confirm that you have found sandstone by doing a simple acid test. If the rock fizzes when you drop a few drops of vinegar, it is likely sandstone.

Sandstone is a rock that stands out due to its unique structure, beautiful colors, and durability. It has been used for centuries in construction, art, and practical purposes and continues to be popular today. If you come across a rock with a rough surface, visible grains of sand, and a layered appearance, it might be sandstone. So, the next time you see an old building made of sandstone or a natural sandstone formation, take a moment to appreciate this rock that stands the test of time.

Siltstone

Have you ever heard of siltstone? This sedimentary rock may not be as well-known as some of the most popular rock types, but it plays an important role in our everyday lives. Siltstone is a versatile rock with various uses, from construction materials to decorative purposes.

Definition of Siltstone

Siltstone is a sedimentary rock composed of silt-sized particles, smaller than sand and larger than clay. This type of rock is formed through sediment accumulation, particularly fine-grained particles such as silt and clay. Siltstone is often found in layers and can have a range of colors, including gray, green, brown, and red.

Structure of Siltstone

Siltstone has a fine-grained structure with closely packed layers of silt-sized particles. The rock has a smooth texture and can have a platey or blocky appearance, depending on how it was formed. Siltstone is not very porous and has a relatively low permeability, meaning it does not allow water to pass through easily. Due to these characteristics, siltstone is often used as a building material for structures that require strong, stable foundations.

Uses of Siltstone

Siltstone has a range of uses in construction, decorative, and industrial applications. It is often used as a building material for walls, floors, and foundations. Siltstone is also used in landscaping and as decorative stones in gardens and outdoor spaces. In industry, rock is used as a raw material for the production of cement and other building materials. Additionally, siltstone can be crushed and used as a soil amendment to improve drainage and aeration in garden beds.

Tips for Identifying Siltstone

If you want to identify siltstone, there are a few key characteristics to look for. Siltstone has a medium to fine-grained texture and often has visible layers or laminations. The rock is dense and hard, with a smooth surface that can be scratched with a knife or nail. Siltstone often has a gray or brown color but can also be green, red, or other shades. In the field, siltstone can be identified by its blocky or platey appearance, and it often breaks into flat, smooth fragments.

Siltstone may not be the most well-known type of rock, but it is an important one with various uses in construction, decorative, and industrial applications. Its fine-grained structure and dense, hard texture make it a strong and stable building material for structures that require a solid foundation. Whether you're a geology enthusiast or just curious about the rocks around you, siltstone is a fascinating type of rock to learn about and appreciate.

Shale

Chances are, if you've heard the word "shale" before, it was probably about the controversial natural gas- and oil-extraction process known as fracking. But shale isn't just a source of fuel. It's a sedimentary rock with a complex structure and a wide range of potential uses. This section will look at the different aspects of shale, from its definition and structure to its various applications and tips for identifying it in the field.

Definition of Shale

Shale is a fine-grained sedimentary rock composed of clay minerals and other inorganic and organic minerals such as quartz, calcite, feldspar, and mica. It forms through the compaction and cementation of clay, silt, and other fine-grained rocks. This process can occur on land (terrestrial shale) and underwater (marine shale). Shale is typically very thin, with a thickness of fewer than two inches, and it can be found in layers within larger formations of rock.

Shale.
https://pixabay.com/es/photos/esquisto-roca-roto-textura-rocoso-2255022/

Structure of Shale

Shale is a layered rock characterized by its fiscality, or ability to split neatly along parallel planes. This distinctive feature results from the clay minerals that make up the bulk of the rock. These minerals tend to align in thin, flat plates that can easily slide past each other. The shale layers can also exhibit a range of other features, such as ripple marks, fossilized marine organisms, and small cracks and faults. These characteristics are key for understanding the depositional environment of the shale and its potential uses.

Uses of Shale

Shale has a variety of applications in industries ranging from construction to energy production to agriculture. Shale is often used as a raw material for manufacturing bricks, tiles, and other ceramic products in the construction industry. It is also used for road construction and as a filler material in concrete. Shale can also be a valuable natural gas and oil source, as mentioned earlier. In agriculture, shale is used as a soil conditioner, as it helps to improve soil drainage and aeration.

Tips for Identifying Shale

Identifying shale in the field can be challenging because it often appears similar to other fine-grained sedimentary rocks like siltstone, mudstone, and shale's cousin, slate. However, some key characteristics can help you differentiate shale from these other rocks. One way to identify shale is to look for its distinctive fiscality. If a rock splits neatly along parallel planes, it's likely shale. Another way to identify shale is to perform a scratch test with a knife. Shale is typically softer than slate and will leave a mark when scratched. In addition, shale often has a dull, flat appearance compared to the shiny, reflective surface of slate.

Shale may have gained notoriety as a source of natural gas and oil through the contentious process of fracking, but its complex structure and diverse applications make it an intriguing and valuable rock for a range of industries. From its fine-grained composition to its distinctive fiscality, shale offers unique opportunities for exploration and exploitation. Whether you're a geologist, a builder, or just a casual rockhound, understanding shale and its many facets can deepen your appreciation for the intricate and ever-evolving world of rocks and minerals.

Sedimentary rocks are a diverse group of rocks formed through the compaction and cementation of loose sediment. These rocks can be divided into clastic, organic, and chemical. Clastic sedimentary rocks are composed of particles of broken-down material from preexisting rocks. Examples of these types of sedimentary rocks include sandstone, conglomerate, shale, and limestone. Organic sedimentary rocks are composed of organic material from living organisms, such as coal and limestone.

Chemical sedimentary rocks form through the precipitation of minerals dissolved in water and can include evaporites like halite and gypsum. The unique characteristics of sedimentary rocks, such as their fiscality and depositional environment, make them incredibly valuable in various industries. As you explore the world of rocks and minerals, take the time to appreciate and understand all of the different types of sedimentary rocks. From sandstone to shale, these remarkable rocks are a testament to the power of nature and its ability to shape our planet.

Chapter 4: Metamorphic Rocks

Did you know that some rocks are transformed from one type to another? This transformation is called metamorphism, and the result of this process is known as a metamorphic rock!

Metamorphic rocks are some of the most interesting and beautiful formations on Earth. From quartzite to marble, schist to gneiss, these rocks have significantly transformed from their original igneous, sedimentary, or even earlier metamorphic form. This chapter will explore more about what metamorphic rocks are and how they form. The two main types of metamorphic rocks and some other notable examples will also be discussed. By the end of this chapter, you should have a good understanding of metamorphic rocks and how to identify them.

What Are Metamorphic Rocks?

The Earth's crust is a fascinating labyrinth filled with an array of minerals, rocks, and sediments that have been formed due to various geological processes over millions of years. Metamorphic rocks are one such type of rock and can be described as any rock that has been substantially changed from its original igneous, sedimentary, or earlier metamorphic form. From marble to quartzite, phyllite to schist, and gneiss to slate, each of these rocks has a unique origin story that is characterized by intense pressure and/or heat.

Definition of Metamorphic Rocks

Metamorphic rocks have been transformed from their original state through heat, pressure, and chemical reactions while still in a solid state. These rocks are formed from preexisting rocks (known as parent rocks or protoliths) subjected to intense pressure and heat from the proximity of magma or another heat source. The extreme temperature and pressure conditions alter the rock's mineral composition, chemical properties, and physical appearance to form metamorphic rocks.

Structure of Metamorphic Rocks

Metamorphic rocks come in different compositions and structures depending on the intensity of the conditions of their formation. They have distinct banding, layering, or a combination of both and can have a variety of mineral orientations. Their texture ranges from coarse to fine, depending on the degree of strain and recrystallization. In some cases, metamorphic rocks preserve the characteristics of the parent rock, such as its fossils, but in most cases, they have a completely different look and feel.

Formation of Metamorphic Rocks

Metamorphic rocks are formed through two processes: regional metamorphism and contact metamorphism. Regional metamorphism happens when rocks are subjected to high pressure and temperature caused by the collision of tectonic plates or when deep-seated rocks are exposed to the Earth's surface. Contact metamorphism occurs when rocks come into contact with magma or any other heat source, causing them to crystallize, recrystallize, and form new minerals. The type of metamorphic rock formed depends on the composition of the parent rock, the duration and intensity of heat and pressure, and the presence of fluids that contribute to the alteration of the minerals.

Metamorphic rocks show the remarkable effects of the enormous forces of heat and pressure on geological materials. They are a fascinating piece of Earth's history and have significant value in a range of areas, including architecture, construction, and sculptures. Understanding the formation and structure of metamorphic rocks offers valuable insights into how the Earth's crust has evolved, the role of tectonic plates in shaping the Earth's surface, and the potential for discoveries. By exploring the world of metamorphic rocks, we get a new appreciation for the planet we inhabit and the forces that created it and are still at work creating it.

Foliated Metamorphic Rocks

If you're a geology enthusiast, you've probably heard of foliated metamorphic rocks. These rocks have unique features that distinguish them from other rock types. But what are they, and what makes them special? This section will explore foliated metamorphic rocks, their characteristics, their different types, and tips for identifying them.

Definition

Foliated rocks are metamorphic rocks with a layered or banded appearance created by high pressure and heat exposure. These rocks share a property called foliation. Foliation is the arrangement of minerals in a metamorphic rock, which creates parallel layers or sheets. These rocks are formed through the process of metamorphism, which occurs when rocks are subjected to high temperatures and pressures caused by tectonic activities like mountain building, contact metamorphism, and regional metamorphism.

Characteristics of Foliated Metamorphic Rocks

One characteristic of foliated metamorphic rocks is the presence of cleavage. Cleavage refers to the ability of a rock to break along flat and parallel surfaces. For example, a schist can easily be broken into thin flat sheets along its cleavage. Other characteristics include the arrangement of specific minerals like mica, chlorite, and hornblende in a layer-like structure that creates a banded appearance. The more intense the pressure and heat, the more pronounced the banding becomes. The grains in these rocks also tend to be elongated or flattened, making them look stretched out.

Types of Foliated Metamorphic Rocks

There are various types of foliated metamorphic rocks, and all differ in their composition and texture. Slate is one such type, which has a fine-grained texture signified by microscopic clay minerals. Phyllite is another type with a shiny appearance with a texture between slate and schist. Schist is the most common type and is characterized by large grains of mica, which gives it a shiny appearance. Gneiss has a coarse texture and is more coarse-grained than schist. Lastly, migmatite is a rare type that forms when a rock undergoes partial melting.

Phyllite.

James St. John, CC BY 2.0 <https://creativecommons.org/licenses/by/2.0>, via Wikimedia Commons https://commons.wikimedia.org/wiki/File:Phyllite_(French_Slate,_Paleoproterozoic;_Snowy_Range_Road_roadcut,_Medicine_Bow_Mountains,_Wyoming,_USA)_8_(45625222381).jpg

Tips for Identifying Foliated Metamorphic Rocks

While identifying foliated metamorphic rocks may seem challenging, there are certain indicators to look out for. One way to identify them is to look for parallel lines or banding in the rock. Other factors to consider include the type of minerals present, the texture of the rock, and the presence of cleavage. Some rocks may also have a shiny or reflective appearance, indicating the presence of mica or other minerals.

Foliated metamorphic rocks offer a fascinating glimpse into the geological history of our planet. These rocks' unique features and composition are a testament to the powerful forces that have shaped our world. By understanding the characteristics, types, and identifying factors of foliated metamorphic rocks, we can appreciate the beauty and complexity of our planet's geology. So, the next time you come across a foliated rock, take a moment to marvel at the natural wonder of it all!

Non-Foliated Metamorphic Rocks

Rocks are some of the oldest materials on our planet Earth. They've been shaped and reshaped over time due to various geological forces. Metamorphic rocks transform form and composition over time due to heat, pressure, and other factors. Non-foliated metamorphic rocks are those rocks that lack a visible alignment of minerals. In simpler terms, they don't have layers. This particular type of metamorphic rock has several characteristics, types, and tips for identifying them.

Definition

Non-foliated metamorphic rocks are rocks that have transformed without producing a layered or banded texture. This means that they have a uniform composition throughout the rock. They typically crystallize under conditions of high pressure and low temperature. Due to their uniform composition, they are often used for building and construction purposes.

Characteristics of Non-Foliated Metamorphic Rocks

Non-foliated metamorphic rocks have several characteristics which set them apart from other forms. For one, these rocks tend to have a lack of visible layers or bands of minerals. They are also generally hard and durable, making them ideal for construction use. Some examples of non-foliated metamorphic rocks include marble, quartzite, and hornfels.

Types of Non-Foliated Metamorphic Rocks

There are several types of non-foliated metamorphic rocks, each with unique composition and characteristics. Marble, for instance, is a non-foliated metamorphic rock composed almost entirely of calcite, a mineral that makes it slightly harder than limestone. On the other hand, quartzite is a metamorphic rock composed almost entirely of quartz grains. And hornfels is a fine-grained metamorphosed rock composed of several different minerals, including quartz, feldspar, and mica.

Quartzite.

James St. John, CC BY 2.0 <https://creativecommons.org/licenses/by/2.0>, via Wikimedia Commons https://commons.wikimedia.org/wiki/File:Sioux_Quartzite_(Paleoproterozoic,_1.65_to_1.70_Ga;_Transcontinental_Arch,_USA)_17.jpg

Tips for Identifying Non-Foliated Metamorphic Rocks

There are a few things to look out for to identify non-foliated metamorphic rocks. One of the most notable things about these rocks is that, unlike foliated metamorphic rocks, they do not have a visible layering or banding of minerals. They also are usually quite hard and durable, which makes them useful for construction. Finally, there is often a uniform texture throughout the rock.

Non-foliated metamorphic rocks are an essential part of our geological history that has shaped our planet. These rocks are incredibly hard and durable, thanks to the transformation they undergo. They don't have layered minerals, offering a uniform texture throughout the rock. This makes them useful for construction and building purposes. Knowing the characteristics, types, and tips to identify them can be helpful to geologists, construction workers, or anyone interested in the Earth's geological history.

Notable Examples of Metamorphic Rocks

Metamorphic rocks provide a unique glimpse into the planet's geologic past, as their original identity has been partially or completely altered. Notable examples of metamorphic rocks include slate, schist, marble, quartzite, and gneiss. All of these metamorphic rocks possess incredible strength due to the changes they undergo during their formation. These rocks' hard, durable qualities make them ideal for various construction and building purposes. They are also popular among collectors and can be found in many homes, offices, and museums.

Marble

Marble is a beautiful and versatile stone widely used for architectural, sculptural, and decorative purposes. The unique characteristics of marble make it a popular choice for homeowners, designers, and builders worldwide. This metamorphic rock is formed by transforming limestone or dolomite through heat and pressure. Stone made from limestone or dolomite has tiny crystals of calcite. It looks different based on what the original rock was made of.

History

Marble has been used since ancient times to symbolize wealth, power, and beauty. The ancient Greeks and Romans built magnificent temples, statues, and buildings with marble, and their art and architecture legacy is still visible today. The world-renowned marble quarries of Carrara, Italy, have operated since Roman times and provided the precious material for masterpieces like Michelangelo's David and the Pantheon in Rome. Today, marble is still quarried in many countries like Italy, Spain, Greece, Turkey, Brazil, and the USA. The rich variety of colors, textures, and marble patterns makes it a favorite among designers and architects.

Marble.

James St. John, CC BY 2.0 <https://creativecommons.org/licenses/by/2.0>, via Wikimedia Commons https://commons.wikimedia.org/wiki/File:Marble_(Murphy_Marble,_Ordovician;_quarry_near_Tate,_Georgia,_USA)_(16268833583).jpg

Properties

The properties of marble make it an excellent choice for many applications. Marble is a durable, heat-resistant stone that can withstand high traffic in areas like bathrooms, kitchens, and floors. Its smooth surface makes it easy to clean and maintain and does not attract bacteria or allergens. Marble is also a popular option for countertops, vanities, and backsplashes because of its resistance to stains and scratches. It can last for decades and improve with age, developing a natural patina that adds to its beauty if cared for properly.

Uses

One of the main attractions of marble is its uniqueness. No two pieces of marble are alike, and the variations in color, pattern, and veining give each slab its character. From the classic white and gray marbles to the exotic green, red, and pink varieties, marble can add elegance and refinement to any space. The popularity of marble has also led to the development of new finishes and treatments that enhance its versatility. Honed or matte finishes are great for a subtle and sophisticated look, while polished or glossy finishes give an irresistible shine.

Care

Caring for marble is essential to maintain its beauty and longevity. Marble is susceptible to etching caused by acidic substances like vinegar, lemon juice, or wine, so avoiding contact with these liquids is essential. It is recommended to clean marble with a pH-neutral cleaner and a soft cloth or sponge. Avoid using abrasive cleaners or scourers that can scratch the stone's surface. Sealing marble is also recommended to prevent stains and water damage. If you notice any cracks or chips in the marble, it is essential to address them promptly to avoid further damage.

Marble is a stunning and fascinating material that has stood the test of time. From ancient origins to modern applications, marble symbolizes beauty, luxury, and elegance. Its unique properties, versatility, and variety make it a favorite among architects, designers, and homeowners worldwide. Caring for marble is essential to ensure its durability and beauty for years to come. Whether you choose classic white marble or exotic green marble, there is no denying that marble is a timeless and exquisite choice.

Quartzite

When it comes to rocks that people know and love, quartzite is not usually the first that comes to mind. Most people have never even heard of it. However, this metamorphic rock deserves some attention for its hidden beauty and unique characteristics.

What Is Quartzite, Exactly?

Quartzite is a metamorphic rock formed when quartz sandstone is exposed to high heat and pressure deep within the Earth's crust. This process causes the sand particles in the rock to recrystallize and fuse, creating a denser and harder rock than the original sandstone. Quartzite is often mistaken for marble or granite because of its glossy surface and vibrant colors.

Characteristics

One of the most notable characteristics of quartzite is its durability. Quartzite is incredibly resistant to wear and tear, unlike other natural stones that can be vulnerable to scratching, staining, and etching. This makes it ideal for kitchen countertops, flooring, and outdoor paving. It is also heat-resistant, so you can place hot pots and pans directly on the surface without fear of damage. With proper care and maintenance, quartzite can last a lifetime.

Advantages

Quartzite is highly sought after for its impressive range of colors and patterns, providing endless design possibilities. Because of the variety of minerals that can be present in the original sandstone, quartzite can come in an array of colors, such as white, gray, pink, and yellow. Some even have unexpected colors like blue and green. The patterns found within the rock can range from subtle grains to bold swirls and veining. This means quartzite can be used in any design style, from traditional to modern.

Despite its many benefits, quartzite is often overlooked in favor of more well-known natural stones like granite and marble. The main reason is the misconception that quartzite is difficult to work with. Quartzite requires some skill and expertise to fabricate and install, but with the help of a professional stone supplier, it can be an easy and stress-free process.

Overall, quartzite is a unique metamorphic rock that deserves more attention in the world of natural stone. With its durability, color range, and hidden beauty, quartzite is a great option for any home renovation project. Don't be afraid to explore this hidden gem and discover how it can enhance your living space.

Phyllite

Nature never ceases to amaze us with its spectacular output. The evolution of rocks is a living example of how every inch of our planet has a unique story to tell. One such rock is phyllite, making its mark among the metamorphic rocks. Found in various parts of the world, phyllite is a rock that has undergone a remarkable transformation from sedimentary or igneous rock to its metamorphic form.

Formation

Phyllite is a metamorphic rock formed from the continual pressure and heat metamorphosing slate, one of the many sedimentary rocks. The process of metamorphosis of phyllite has gone through various phases, resulting in its distinct texture and beautiful appearance. One can experience the beauty of phyllite by examining it closely, touching its smooth surface, and peering into its mica crystals. The mica crystals are responsible for the sheen and shine, while chlorite crystals lend it its beautiful green color.

Characteristics

Phyllite rocks' unique texture lies in their appearance, which resembles closely stacked fan-like shapes formed due to their frequent layers. These layers result from the repeated compression and flattening of the sedimentary rock when metamorphosing into phyllite. Owing to its texture, it has become an excellent building material in countries such as Germany, where it has found its application in renowned structures.

Phyllite rock plays a crucial role in Earth's ancient history's chemical, physical, and geological studies. It contains essential minerals like garnet, staurolite, and biotite, which help when studying the Earth's past. Scientists can determine which group of rocks was present during the formation of Phyllite, which can provide insight into the time several rocks in that region were created.

Uses

Phyllite's durability and hardness make it an excellent building and flooring material, primarily when it is present in layers. Apart from building materials, it is also used in electrical engineering, synthetic diamond manufacturing, and cosmetic products manufacturing.

Phyllite's beauty speaks for itself and its significance in Earth's natural history. It is a product of nature's magic and evolution. Phyllite's unique texture and composition make it an excellent choice for various applications, from decorative tiles to scientific research. Its charm and relevance continue to amaze geologists, archaeologists, and common folk alike. So, the next time you stumble upon a phyllite rock, take a moment to acknowledge its magic and wonder.

Schist

Nature is a masterful artist, and some of its finest masterpieces come in the form of metamorphic rocks. Schist is one such rock that has piqued the interest of geologists, collectors, and enthusiasts alike. Schist rocks are some of the most beautiful geological specimens with their sparkling appearance and intricate patterns.

Schist.
James St. John, CC BY 2.0 <https://creativecommons.org/licenses/by/2.0>, via Wikimedia Commons https://commons.wikimedia.org/wiki/File:Garnet-chlorite_schist_(Lake_Martin,_Alabama,_USA)_2_(33367535678).jpg

Formation

Schist is a metamorphic rock that forms from preexisting rocks due to heat and pressure. As the rocks are subjected to high pressure and high temperature, the minerals inside them start to recrystallize and align themselves along parallel planes. This process leads to the formation of the distinct banding and foliation characteristic of Schist. The heat and pressure levels required for schist to form are higher than that required to form slate but lower than that required for gneiss.

Types

Schist comes in various types, depending on the rock from which it is formed and the minerals that are present in it. The most common types of Schist are mica-schist, garnet-schist, and talc-schist. Mica-schist is the most recognizable due to its distinctive shiny appearance caused by the presence of mica minerals. Garnet-schist is another type that is recognizable due to the presence of garnet, which gives it a reddish color. Talc-schist, on the other hand, is created from the metamorphism of ultramafic rocks, and it has a greasy texture due to the high presence of talc.

Uses

Schist is a sought-after rock for collectors and enthusiasts because of its beauty and rarity. Its varied types and patterns make it a visual delight as well as a collector's dream. Furthermore, schist is also used for several practical applications. The rock's banded and foliated structure makes it a popular choice for decorative stones, while its high resistance to wear and tear makes it ideal for use in flooring, countertops, and roofing.

Schist is a stunning and versatile rock that can be appreciated for its aesthetic and practical features. Its glittering appearance and formations illustrate the extraordinary abilities of our planet's natural processes. Schist's usefulness and beauty have made it an object of human fascination for centuries, and its allure continues to enchant people today. So, the next time you admire a schist formation, you can marvel at the fascinating geological processes that shaped and gave birth to these stunning jewels of the Earth.

Gneiss

Rocks have been around us for millions of years, and metamorphic rocks, in particular, are fascinating because they are formed through the transformation of rocks. One such type of rock that deserves attention is gneiss. Gneiss is a metamorphic rock with a layered structure composed of different minerals.

Gneiss.
James St. John, CC BY 2.0 <https://creativecommons.org/licenses/by/2.0>, via Wikimedia Commons https://commons.wikimedia.org/wiki/File:Gneiss_2_(33239757534).jpg

What Is Gneiss?

Gneiss is a metamorphic rock formed through the process of metamorphism. It is a combination of different minerals compressed together during high-pressure and high-temperature conditions, which change the rock's original structure. Gneiss's strong foliation or layering makes it distinguishable from other metamorphic rocks.

How Is Gneiss Formed?

Gneiss is formed through metamorphism, where rocks undergo immense heat and pressure. The parent rocks of gneiss are usually igneous or sedimentary rocks subjected to metamorphic processes. These processes include regional and contact metamorphisms, where rocks experience high temperatures and pressure due to movements in the Earth's crust. This causes the minerals within the rock to change and combine to form gneiss.

Different Types of Gneiss

Gneiss is a complex rock, which means it has different types based on the minerals present. The most common type is biotite gneiss, which has a layer of biotite mineral sandwiched between two layers of feldspar. Another type is granitic gneiss, composed of granite minerals such as quartz, feldspar, and mica. Similarly, mafic gneiss is composed of dark minerals like hornblende and pyroxene.

Uses of Gneiss

Gneiss has many uses because of its unique properties. It is often used in construction as a decorative stone because of its different colors and patterns. Gneiss can be polished to a high luster, making it attractive as a building material. In addition, gneiss is used as a dimension stone, making it ideal for cut and design purposes. Given its durability and strength, Gneiss can also be used to create beautiful countertops, flooring tiles, and walls. Gneiss is commonly used for walkways, outdoor sculptures, and garden beds in landscaping. Additionally, this rock can be crushed and used as ballast, concrete aggregate, or railroad track materials.

Gneiss is a fascinating metamorphic rock with a unique structure and diverse uses. Its composition and properties make it a valuable rock in various industries, and its beauty makes it a choice building material for construction purposes. With its durability and decorative properties, gneiss is not just a rock but a work of art that time and pressure have created.

Metamorphic rocks are a very visible reminder of the power of nature and the Earth's ability to transform what was once thought to be nothing into something beautiful and valuable. The types of metamorphic rocks discussed in this chapter have become a staple in many industries as people have found ways to utilize their unique properties. From construction to landscaping, these rocks deserve recognition and admiration. With their incredible strength and beauty, it's no wonder that metamorphic rocks have become so popular.

Chapter 5: Minerals and Crystal Systems

Minerals are remarkable substances that can form into many shapes and sizes. What's even more amazing is their underlying structure, which scientists have long studied in detail by scientists. Minerals follow organized patterns known as crystal systems, each with unique characteristics. For example, the cubic system has equal lengths on each side to form a perfect cube, while other systems feature less perfect shapes, such as hexagons and prisms.

Whether you are just beginning to learn or already adept at identifying them, minerals offer something for everyone to explore through crystal systems. This chapter will cover how minerals are classified, the different types, and their associated crystal systems. Some of the properties of minerals and how to use them for identification will also be touched upon. By the end, you'll be able to look at a mineral specimen and identify its crystal system.

Minerals and Crystals

Regarding geology and mineralogy, minerals and crystals are the building blocks of everything we see around us. They are the natural components that make up the Earth's crust and form the bedrock of geological processes. Minerals exhibit a variety of structures and physical properties, and their importance in various fields, including industrial applications, medicine, and nanotechnology, cannot be overstated. This section will explore the world of minerals and crystals and understand their significance in geology and mineralogy.

Minerals and Their Formation

Minerals are naturally occurring inorganic solids with a defined chemical composition and a distinct crystal structure. They are formed through various geological processes, such as crystal precipitation from molten lava or groundwater solutions, a chemical reaction between different minerals, and metamorphic changes resulting from heat and pressure. Key properties of minerals include color, hardness, cleavage, and luster, which help geologists identify and classify minerals.

Types of Crystals and Their Properties

Crystals are the repeating structure of atoms in a mineral, giving it its distinctive shape and properties. Different types of crystals exhibit varying levels of symmetry and complexity. The seven crystal systems, including cubic, tetragonal, orthorhombic, monoclinic, triclinic, hexagonal, and rhombohedral, are based on the axial length and angle of the crystal structure. Each system has its particular characteristics, such as optical, magnetic properties, and piezoelectricity.

Significance of Minerals

Minerals have a wide range of industrial applications, from manufacturing materials like ceramics, glass, and cement to electronic devices like transistors, batteries, and superconductors. They are also essential for advanced technologies like solar panels, wind turbines, and electric vehicle batteries. Some minerals like gold, iron, and copper have been used as currency and traded for thousands of years.

Mineral Exploration and Mining

Mineral exploration involves finding and identifying mineral deposits in the Earth's crust. Geologists use various techniques such as geological mapping, geochemical analysis, and remote sensing to locate minerals. Once mineral deposits are discovered, they can be mined, which involves the extraction of ore from the ground and processing it to extract the mineral of interest. Mining can have significant environmental impacts, and sustainable mining practices are essential to minimize these impacts.

Importance of Conservation and Sustainability

Given the finite nature of mineral resources, sustainable mining practices are becoming increasingly essential to minimize the impact of mining on the environment and the surrounding communities. However, conservation practices are equally crucial, as they help preserve the Earth's natural resources and ensure their availability for future generations.

Minerals and crystals are the foundation of geology and mineralogy, and their importance in various fields cannot be overstated. Understanding their properties and structures is essential for their identification, classification, and use in a wide range of applications while ensuring sustainable mining practices and conservation efforts will help in preserving these natural resources for the future.

Types of Minerals

Minerals are essential elements in our planet's crust, formed over millions of years by different geological processes. They play a crucial role in the formation of rocks, soils, and natural resources, as well as being vital for our health and well-being. With over 5,000 identified minerals, we have compiled the eight main types of minerals that are commonly found on Earth. Join us in discovering each mineral's unique features and importance in our daily lives.

1. **Silicates:** This type of mineral is the most abundant and flexible of all minerals, with silicon and oxygen being the most prominent components. Silicates comprise over 90% of the Earth's crust, with quartz being the most common mineral. They are used in a wide range of applications like construction, electronics, and silicon chips and are essential for human health.

2. **Oxides:** Oxides combine oxygen with metals like iron, copper, and aluminum to create valuable resources like iron ore and aluminum ore. These minerals are crucial in industries like construction and manufacturing. The most common oxide is corundum, the base mineral for rubies and sapphires. In nature, it is often found in the form of dust or sand.

3. **Sulfates:** Sulfates are minerals that contain sulfur, water, and metals like copper, zinc, and iron. Gypsum is an example of a sulfate mineral and is commonly used in the construction industry to create plaster and drywall. Sulfate minerals also play an important role in forming soil and water quality. The

most common sulfate mineral is barite, which can be found in large deposits worldwide. In addition, it is used in a wide range of industrial applications.

4. **Sulfides**: Sulfides are minerals that contain sulfur and metals like lead, gold, silver, and copper. These minerals are the primary source of many metal ores, like zinc ore and copper ore, and have significant economic value. While sulfides are essential for extracting valuable metals, they can also be toxic and hazardous to our environment. The most commonly found sulfide mineral is pyrite, which is also known as fool's gold.

5. **Halides**: Halides are minerals formed when halogen elements like chlorine, fluorine, and iodine combine with metals like sodium, potassium, and calcium. Halite or rock salt is a common halide mineral used in the food industry and can be found in natural salt deposits. Its high chlorine content is also used in industrial processes like water treatment and wastewater management. The most common halide mineral is fluorite, a valuable fluoride source for dental health.

6. **Carbonates:** Carbonates contain carbon and oxygen, with minerals like calcite and dolomite being the most common. These minerals are significant in the formation of natural habitats like caves and coral reefs, as well as being an essential ingredient in concrete and cement. The most common carbonate mineral is calcite, which is composed of calcium and magnesium. With its high calcium content, it is often used as a dietary supplement in the form of limestone. The mineral is also used in the production of marble and glass.

7. **Phosphates**: Phosphates are minerals containing phosphate and oxygen, with apatite being the most common example. Phosphate fertilizers are widely used in agriculture to enhance plant growth, and phosphate minerals also play a crucial role in human bone formation. Phosphate is also used in laundry detergents and toothpaste to help remove food stains. The most common phosphate mineral is monazite, which contains rare Earth elements and is used in electronics production.

8. **Native Elements:** Native elements are minerals that naturally exist without combining with other elements, like gold, platinum, and silver. These minerals have significant economic value in the jewelry industry and have been used extensively throughout history as a form of currency. Some native elements, like silver and gold, are also used in electronics and dentistry. The most common native element is quartz, composed of silicon and oxygen. Quartz is often used in clocks, watches, and microchips.

The world of minerals is fascinating and diverse, and they play an essential role in our daily lives. The eight primary mineral types offer crucial resources that have shaped our civilization, from building materials to food ingredients and electronics to jewelry. Understanding the importance of minerals and their uses can help us appreciate their value and encourage their sustainable use. With discoveries of new minerals being made every day, we can expect to learn more about the unique features and importance of these valuable resources.

Crystal Systems

Crystals are fascinating to look at and hold. From their exquisite beauty to their unique properties, crystals have been used for decorative and spiritual purposes for centuries. One thing that makes crystals so intriguing is the different ways they can grow and form. This section will explore the six different types of crystal systems, including isometric, tetragonal, orthorhombic, hexagonal, monoclinic, and triclinic. Let's dive in!

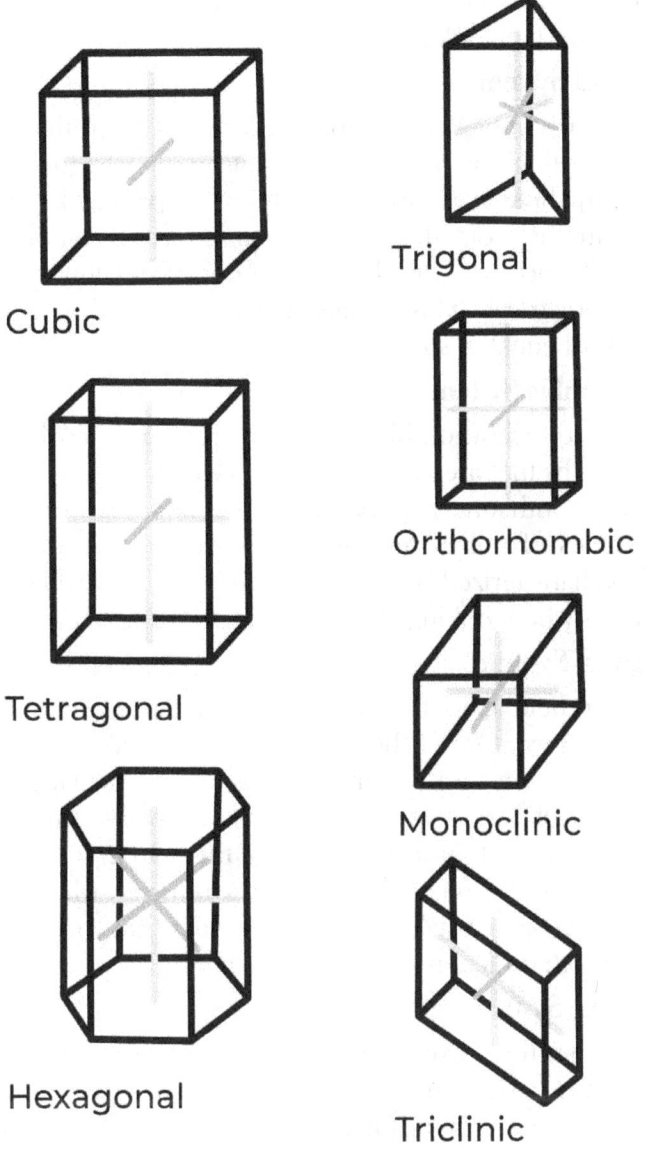

The 6 main crystal systems.

1. Isometric System

The isometric system, also known as the cubic system, is characterized by crystals with three axes intersecting at 90 degrees, equal length, and perpendicular to each other. The most common example of this system is the diamond. Other examples include galena, pyrite, fluorite, and garnet. The working of this system is based on the fact that all faces and angles are equal. You will see an identical pattern regardless of which direction you look at the crystal.

2. Tetragonal System

This system resembles the isometric system, except that one axis is longer or shorter than the other two. Crystals in the tetragonal system are characterized by three axes, two of which are perpendicular while one is inclined. Examples of this system are zircon, cassiterite, and chalcopyrite. Characterized by elongation in one direction, the tetragonal system is asymmetrical. This means that the faces of a crystal in this system are not all equal in size.

3. Orthorhombic System

Crystals in the orthorhombic system are characterized by three axes of different lengths that are all at right angles to each other. They are not equal in length, with one axis being shorter and the other two being longer. Examples of this system are topaz, barite, and aragonite. This system is also characterized by a lack of symmetry. You will see different faces and angles when looking at a crystal from this system.

4. Hexagonal System

Crystals that belong to the hexagonal system have four axes that define their structure. Out of these, three are of equal length and at 120 degrees to each other, and a fourth axis is perpendicular to the other three. Examples of this system include quartz, beryl, and tourmaline. Due to the presence of four axes, crystals in this system have a hexagonal shape. This system is also characterized by symmetry, which means that when looking at the crystal, you will see identical faces and angles regardless of which direction you are looking at it.

5. Monoclinic System

This system has three axes of different lengths, two of which intersect at an oblique angle, while the third is perpendicular to both. Crystals in this system often have a distinguishing incline, making them easily identifiable. Examples of this system include gypsum, azurite, and epidote. This system has the distinctive characteristic of having two axes of different lengths, giving crystals in this system a characteristic asymmetry.

6. Triclinic System

Crystals in this system are the most irregular, with three unequal-length axes intersecting at oblique angles. They're often called *pinacoids* because their irregular shape looks like it has been pinched at the top. Examples of this system include feldspars, kyanite, and labradorite. Apart from their asymmetrical shape, crystals in this system are also characterized by the fact that no two faces of the crystal will ever be parallel. In other words, all faces and angles of the crystal in this system will be unique.

Understanding the different crystal systems and how they form is important for anyone interested in working with or collecting crystals. By knowing which system a crystal belongs to, we can better understand how it may form and what properties it may possess. From the isometric system of diamonds to the triclinic system of feldspars and labradorite, each type of crystal system offers a unique way of understanding the beauty and magic of crystals.

Properties of Minerals

Minerals are the building blocks of the Earth, and understanding their properties is vital when studying geology, mineralogy, and gemology. A mineral is defined as a naturally occurring inorganic solid with a crystalline structure and specific chemical composition. Each mineral has a set of properties unique to its chemical composition and crystalline structure. This section will discuss four fundamental properties of minerals: hardness, diaphaneity, cleavage, and piezoelectricity.

Hardness

The hardness of a mineral is its ability to resist scratching. The Mohs Scale of Hardness, named after the German mineralogist Friedrich Mohs, is the most widely used method for measuring a mineral's hardness. The scale ranges from 1 to 10, with 1 being the softest mineral, talc, and 10 being the hardest, diamond. In between, minerals such as quartz, feldspar, and topaz fall at different hardness levels. Hardness is an essential property for mineral identification, and this information is crucial in fields such as mining and mineral exploration.

Diaphaneity

Diaphaneity refers to a mineral's ability to transmit light. Minerals can be classified as transparent, translucent, or opaque. Diamonds are an excellent example of a mineral with high diaphaneity, as they transmit most of the visible light spectrum. Translucent minerals such as agate allow some light to pass through, while opaque minerals like hematite do not. Diaphaneity affects a mineral's value, especially in the precious gemstone industry, where transparency and clarity are highly coveted.

Cleavage

Cleavage is a mineral's tendency to break along planes of weakness, which leaves a clean break in smooth surfaces. The number and angle of these planes of weakness are specific to each mineral. For example, mica has perfect cleavage, meaning it breaks easily along thin, flat sheets. On the other hand, Feldspar has two planes of cleavage at right angles, resulting in a blocky shape when broken. Understanding cleavage is critical for mineral identification, as it can provide clues to the mineral's crystal structure and chemical composition.

Piezoelectricity

Piezoelectricity refers to a mineral's ability to generate an electric charge when subjected to mechanical stress, such as pressure. Some minerals can produce an electric field when subjected to strain, and vice versa, due to the asymmetrical arrangement of atoms within their crystal structure. Quartz is one such mineral that exhibits strong piezoelectric properties, making it useful in electronic devices such as watches and oscillators.

Understanding the properties of minerals is crucial in many fields, from mining to jewelry-making. Hardness, diaphaneity, cleavage, and piezoelectricity are fundamental properties to consider when studying minerals. As beginners, acquiring knowledge of these mineral properties opens up a whole new world of wonder, especially when exploring the many beautiful minerals found around the world.

The Magic of Minerals and Crystal Systems

If you have ever been fascinated by the beauty and mystery of crystals and minerals, you're certainly not alone. For thousands of years, cultures worldwide have revered these geological wonders for their mystical and healing properties. But aside from their allure and intrigue, minerals and crystals are also used as scientific tools for understanding the Earth's history and its processes. Let's delve deeper into the world of minerals and crystal systems and discover the magic behind these amazing substances!

Aesthetic Properties

One of the most interesting aspects of minerals and crystals is their ability to reflect light. This is known as their optical properties and can reveal a lot about their structure and composition. One property, known as birefringence, causes minerals to split light into two rays, revealing stunning patterns and colors when viewed through a microscope. Other properties, such as fluorescence and phosphorescence, cause minerals to emit light when exposed to certain wavelengths, creating a glowing effect that appears almost magical.

Healing Properties

Aside from their aesthetic properties, many minerals and crystals are also believed to have healing properties. This practice, known as crystal healing, is based on the idea that each crystal emits a unique energy or vibration that can interact with the body's energy field to promote physical and emotional well-being. While there is not yet any scientific evidence to support this practice, many people swear by the transformative effects of crystal healing.

Minerals and crystal systems are fascinating entities that hold a great deal of scientific and cultural significance. Whether you're drawn to their aesthetic beauty, their metaphysical properties, or their scientific value, there is no denying the magic and wonder of these amazing geological wonders. So next time you come across a glittering crystal or a unique mineral, take a moment to appreciate its beauty and all that it represents. Who knows what mysteries and secrets it may hold?

Chapter 6: Quartz

If you're at all interested in geology, you've likely heard that quartz is one of the most abundant minerals in the Earth's crust. It's estimated that quartz makes up around 12% of the Earth's surface. But what exactly is quartz, where is it found, and why is it so common? Quartz is a mineral composed of silicon and oxygen atoms with the chemical formula SiO_2. It comes in many different varieties, including clear quartz, rose quartz, amethyst, and citrine, to name a few. This chapter will explore everything you need to know about this fascinating mineral. By the end of it, you'll have a better understanding of quartz and its many uses.

Fun fact: Quartz crystals can generate electricity when pressure is applied to them. This is known as the piezoelectric effect.

Quartz's Abundance

So, why is quartz so common? One reason is that it forms under a wide range of conditions. It's one of the few minerals that can form at all temperatures and pressures within the Earth's crust. Quartz is most commonly formed in igneous and metamorphic rocks but can also be found in sedimentary rocks. Additionally, quartz is resistant to weathering and erosion, meaning it can survive for long periods and be transported long distances by wind or water. These factors all make quartz one of Earth's most widely distributed minerals.

Another reason for quartz's abundance is its industrial uses. Quartz's unique properties, such as its hardness, chemical stability, and piezoelectricity, make it useful in various industries. For example, quartz is used to manufacture glass, ceramics, semiconductors, and even watches. It's also commonly used as an abrasive in sandpaper and other materials.

Quartz is found worldwide, but certain regions are particularly known for their abundance of quartz. One of the most famous is the Ouachita Mountains in Arkansas, where you can find clear quartz crystals up to a foot long. Brazil is also a major quartz source, with large amethyst and citrine deposits. Other areas where quartz can be found include Madagascar, Namibia, and the Alps in Europe.

Clear Quartz: The Most Versatile Stone

Clear quartz is a perfect choice if you're searching for a versatile stone that adds beauty, balance, and harmony to your life. This enchanting crystal is the most common mineral on Earth and can be found in different places worldwide. Clear quartz has a plethora of wonderful benefits and is treasured in the world of metaphysics. It's no wonder that spiritualists and crystal healers worldwide love this stone.

Characteristics

Clear quartz is a colorless, transparent, six-sided crystal with a prism-like structure. It's known as the "master healer," and it amplifies vibrations around it. Clear quartz is an excellent energy conductor. Thus, it's a stone that enhances spiritual awareness and clarity of thought. Clear quartz's energy encourages thought clarity, spiritual transformation, and overall well-being. It also dilutes negativity and transmutes it into positive energy.

Structure

Clear quartz crystals have a hexagonal structure, which means that each face of the crystal has six sides. Due to the consistency of its six-sided symmetry, it's easy to recognize this crystal. Clear quartz crystals have carefully arranged atoms, forming a lattice grid, which is how the vibrational energy travels through them. The lattice grid arrangements allow clear quartz to store, transmit, amplify, and transform energies.

Hardness

Clear quartz has a hardness rating of 7 on the Mohs Scale of Hardness, making it quite durable. This scale ranges from one to 10, with one being the softest and 10 being the hardest. Clear quartz's durability is essential when using it for daily wear and is perfect for making crystal rings, necklaces, and other jewelry.

Ways to Identify

Clear quartz is relatively easy to identify as it's transparent and colorless. It is non-magnetic and doesn't conduct electricity, so it won't interfere with magnets or conduct electricity. When held under bright light, clear quartz may project a rainbow of colors, which makes it even more captivating.

Clear quartz crystals are an extraordinary gift to humanity from the Earth's womb. Its healing properties make it popular for spiritual awakening and raising vibrations. Clear quartz is simple yet powerful and can greatly help focus and mental clarity. Overall, the world's love for clear quartz is not without reason, as it's a versatile stone in its vibrational properties, resilience, and beauty which make it one of the most beloved stones in the crystal kingdom.

Rose Quartz: A Gemstone with Many Benefits

Rose quartz is a beautiful, semi-precious gemstone found in abundance around the world. It has many qualities that make it highly sought after for its beauty and healing powers. From its lovely pink color to its heartwarming energy, rose quartz is a stone that has been used for centuries in a variety of ways.

Rose Quartz.
James St. John, CC BY 2.0 <https://creativecommons.org/licenses/by/2.0>, via Wikimedia Commons https://commons.wikimedia.org/wiki/File:Rose_quartz_(32132819430).jpg

Characteristics

Rose quartz ranges in color from pale pink to deep rose. Its color comes from traces of titanium, iron, or manganese. The most desirable shade is a pure, slightly pink color, free of any orange or gray hues. It has a vitreous or glassy luster and is translucent to opaque. The stone is highly prized for its color, associated with love and passion. It is often used in jewelry, especially in necklaces and bracelets.

Structure

Rose quartz is a member of the quartz family of minerals, which includes other well-known stones such as amethyst, citrine, and smoky quartz. It's a silicon dioxide mineral, a hexagonal crystal system, and a pyramidal termination. It contains tiny inclusions of pink fibers or needles, which give it a unique look.

Hardness

Rose quartz has a hardness of seven on the Mohs scale, which means that it is relatively hard and durable. It can be scratched by harder minerals such as topaz, sapphire, and diamond. Remember that while rose quartz is hard, it can still be chipped or damaged if exposed to extreme heat or pressure.

Ways to Identify

Color and structure are the ways in which this stone is identified. It should be pale to deep pink without any gray or orange inclusions. It should also have a hexagonal shape and pyramidal termination. You can also use a loupe or magnifying glass to look for inclusions in the stone. It is worth noting that synthetic rose quartz is also available on the market, so purchasing from a reputable dealer is crucial.

Benefits

Rose quartz is known for opening the heart and healing emotional wounds. It is often used in meditation to promote love, compassion, and peace. It is also believed to have physical benefits such as improving circulation, reducing wrinkles, and easing tension headaches. Rose quartz is a versatile stone that can help promote emotional and physical health.

Rose quartz is a beautiful gemstone with many benefits. It has a lovely pink color and heartwarming energy that make it highly prized in the jewelry world. Its hexagonal structure and pyramidal termination make it easy to identify, and its hardness ensures that it will last for many years.

Whether you are seeking emotional healing or physical health benefits, rose quartz is a stone that can help you achieve your goals.

The Magic of Amethyst

Amethyst is one of the most fascinating stones known to man. Its unique purple color and spiritual associations have given it a special place in mystical history as both a decorative stone and a healing crystal. They can be found worldwide, but some of the most ancient and revered specimens have come from Southern Brazil, Uruguay, Madagascar, and Zambia.

Amethyst.
James St. John, CC BY 2.0 <https://creativecommons.org/licenses/by/2.0>, via Wikimedia Commons https://commons.wikimedia.org/wiki/File:Amethyst_(purple_quartz)_15.jpg

Characteristics

Amethyst belongs to the mineral quartz group. It's sometimes called the "Stone of Spirit" because of its spiritual and calming properties. The color can range from pale lilac to deep purple, and it often features natural color zoning. Amethyst is known for its high purity, and it doesn't contain any visible inclusions or impurities. It's also a relatively common mineral, with sizable deposits found all over the world.

Structure

Amethyst has a trigonal crystal system, which forms six-sided prisms with pointed tips. It has a hexagonal, prism-shaped lattice structure that gives it its unique and iconic look. This structure makes it easy to identify, and once you've seen one, you'll have no trouble recognizing amethyst ever again.

Hardness

The hardness of amethyst is seven on the Mohs Hardness Scale. This means it's a relatively durable stone that will resist scratching and wear normally. However, it's still vulnerable to more extreme shocks and scratching from harder materials. So, if you're looking to wear an amethyst ring or pendant, avoiding activities that could put it at risk is best.

Ways to Identify

One of the easiest ways to identify an amethyst is by its color. If you see a purple crystal that's translucent to opaque, then it's worth further investigation. Some other characteristics you should look for in an amethyst include its refractive index, birefringence, and its pleochroism. Amethyst also has a specific gravity of 2.66, which can be used to distinguish it from other minerals.

Amethyst is a beautiful and highly sought-after stone that has fascinated people for centuries. Its unique purple color and spiritual properties have made it a popular choice for jewelry, home decor, and meditation. Hopefully, the in-depth exploration of amethyst's characteristics, structure, hardness, and ways to identify it have given you greater insight and a newfound respect for this incredible stone. If you've never owned an amethyst before, maybe it's time to treat yourself to one and experience its magic for yourself.

Smoky Quartz

Are you looking for a crystal that can help you stay grounded and focused while also providing protection? Look no further than smoky quartz. This beautiful crystal is known for its unique color and powerful properties. In this section, we'll explore smoky quartz's characteristics, structure, and hardness and ways to identify it. By the end, you'll have a greater appreciation for the many benefits of this special crystal.

Smokey quartz.
Rob Lavinsky, CC BY 3.0 <https://creativecommons.org/licenses/by/3.0>, via Wikimedia Commons https://commons.wikimedia.org/wiki/File:Smoky-quartz-TUCQTZ09-03-arkenstone-irocks.png

Characteristics

Smoky quartz is a variety of macrocrystalline quartz that ranges in color from a light gray to a deep, rich brown. Its color comes from the presence of aluminum impurities in the crystal structure. Smoky quartz is known for its transparency and is often found in clusters or as individual crystals. It is also said to have a powerful grounding energy.

Structure

Smoky quartz has a hexagonal crystal system and is composed of silicon dioxide. Its chemical formula is $SiO2$. The crystal structure of smoky quartz is formed by the orderly arrangement of atoms and molecules that make up the crystal lattice. This crystal system is what gives smoky quartz its unique properties and energy.

Hardness

On the Mohs scale of mineral hardness, smoky quartz has a rating of seven. This means that it is relatively hard and durable, making it suitable for many different uses. Smoky quartz is often used in jewelry because of its beauty and durability. It is also used in various industrial applications, such as in high-precision optics.

Ways to Identify

Smoky quartz is identified by its characteristic color, transparency, and crystal structure. It is often found in clusters or as individual crystals. Smoky quartz can also be distinguished from other types of quartz by its brownish-gray color and its unique energy properties. When held, smoky quartz is said to provide a sense of calm and grounding.

Uses

Smoky quartz has many different uses, from jewelry to industrial applications. It is also often used in meditation to help promote a sense of calm and focus. It is also believed to provide protection from negative energy and to ground the wearer. Smoky quartz is also used in various healing modalities, such as crystal healing and Reiki.

Smoky quartz is a powerful and versatile crystal that offers many benefits to its users. From its unique color and structure to its powerful energy properties, it is an excellent choice for those who are looking to stay grounded and focused while also staying protected from negative energy. Whether used in jewelry, meditation, or healing, smoky quartz will surely provide you the benefits you're looking for.

Herkimer Diamond: A Rare Gem

Herkimer diamond is a unique mineral that is found in Herkimer County, New York. These rare gemstones are not diamonds but are quartz crystals that resemble diamonds. They are often used in jewelry making and have become increasingly popular over recent years.

Herkimer diamond.

James St. John, CC BY 2.0 <https://creativecommons.org/licenses/by/2.0>, via Wikimedia Commons https://commons.wikimedia.org/wiki/File:Quartz_(%22Herkimer_Diamond%22)_(near_Herkimer,_New_Y ork_State,_USA)_8.jpg

Characteristics

One of the most significant characteristics of the Herkimer diamond is its clarity. These quartz crystals are known to be very clear, and they are often found in pairs with perfectly symmetrical shapes. Herkimer diamonds are also double-terminated, meaning that they have two terminations, or points, on each end. This characteristic makes them unique compared to other quartz crystals.

Structure

The structure of Herkimer diamond is one of the things that make this mineral different from other quartz crystals. They have a hexagonal crystal system and belong to the trigonal crystal class. The crystal lattice of the Herkimer diamond is also unique because it is structurally perfect. The absence of any inclusion or impurity makes them one of the most beautiful crystals in nature.

Hardness

Herkimer diamond has a hardness level of seven-and-a-half to eight on the Mohs hardness scale. This makes it a very durable mineral and resistant to scratches. It also means that it can be used in jewelry for daily wear with minimal care. The durability of Herkimer diamond also makes it a popular choice for industrial applications such as optical devices.

Ways to Identify

There are several ways to identify Herkimer diamonds. The first is its double-terminated shape, which is unique compared to other quartz crystals. Another way is the clarity of the crystal. Herkimer diamonds are known for their excellent transparency and are often used as a substitute for diamonds. Finally, Herkimer diamonds are specific to Herkimer County in New York. Therefore, if you discover a clear double-terminated quartz crystal outside this region, it is unlikely to be a Herkimer diamond.

Herkimer diamond is a unique and rare mineral with several characteristics that set it apart from other quartz crystals. Its clarity, perfect structure, and double-terminated shape make it a sought-after gemstone for jewelry making. The fact that it is exclusive to a single region in New York also adds to its appeal to rock collectors. There are several ways to identify Herkimer diamonds, including their signature double-termination and crystal clarity. If you ever have the chance to hold a Herkimer diamond, you will appreciate it for its beauty, rarity, and history.

The Lustrous World of Aventurine

Glistening with radiant beauty, aventurine is a sparkling gemstone that arouses the senses of anyone who lays their eyes on it. Whether you're a gem collector or a jewelry lover, aventurine is an irresistible gemstone to which you will find yourself drawn. With its sparkling characteristics, structure, and hardness, aventurine has become one of the world's most valued and sought-after gemstones.

Aventurine.
Mahdikarimi70, CC BY-SA 4.0 <https://creativecommons.org/licenses/by-sa/4.0>, via Wikimedia Commons
https://commons.wikimedia.org/wiki/File:%D8%B3%D9%86%DA%AF_%D8%AF%D9%84%D8%B1%D8%A8%D8%A7-Aventurine_01.jpg

Characteristics

Aventurine is a member of the quartz family and is known for its shimmering luster and captivating sparkles. The stone resembles marble and has a shiny, rainbow color. This is because it contains tiny pieces of fuchsite or mica. These minerals refract light which gives aventurine its distinctive glow. Depending on the number of mineral deposits, aventurine comes in a range of colors, including green, yellow, orange, blue, and red. It is also commonly found with black, gray, and white patterns running through it.

Structure

The structure of aventurine is crystalline, and its lattice is hexagonal. Its six-sided prism shape gives it a distinct geometric appearance, which makes it easily recognizable. The lattice structure in aventurine is what gives it its hardness and durability, making it perfect for carving and creating jewelry. The hexagonal arrangement of atoms gives aventurine its strength, meaning it can withstand daily wear and tear without cracking or breaking.

Hardness

Aventurine is a moderately hard gemstone with a Mohs hardness scale in the range of six-and-a-half to seven. However, its hardness can vary slightly depending on the color and quality of the stone. For instance, aventurine with more mica flakes or mineral deposits tends to be slightly softer than those with fewer deposits. Nevertheless, aventurine is still one of the most durable gemstones in the quartz family.

Ways to Identify

To accurately recognize aventurine, look for its unique color, inspect the structure of the stone, and gauge its hardness. Its characteristic luster and sparkle are a dead giveaway that its aventurine. When you hold it up to the light, it should also have a translucent quality, with its internal inclusions and mineral deposits visible. Additionally, its relatively high density can differentiate aventurine from glass or plastic stones.

Aventurine is a gemstone that adds a touch of glimmer to any piece of jewelry or collection. With its brilliant shine, unique characteristics, and durability, it's no wonder that aventurine has become a favorite choice amongst gem enthusiasts. Its hexagonal lattice structure and crystalline framework make it innovative and adaptable. Additionally, inclusions and mineral deposits tend to give it a natural and organic feel. When identifying an aventurine, look for its unique glow and hexagonal structure. If you're looking for a gemstone that possesses unparalleled splendor and remarkable durability, aventurine is a perfect choice.

Exploring the Alluring World of Citrine

If you're a fan of gemstones, you must have heard of citrine. This golden-colored crystal is adored for its beauty and energy-healing properties. But what exactly is citrine? Where does it come from? How can you identify it? From the characteristics of citrine to its structure and ways to identify it, we've got you covered. So, let's dive into the alluring world of citrine.

Citrine.
https://pixabay.com/es/photos/citrino-cristal-roca-cuarzo-joya-1093454/

Characteristics

Citrine, a popular variety of quartz, is a yellow to golden-orange-colored gemstone. Citrine's unique color comes from the iron present in its crystal structure. It is found in many countries worldwide, including Brazil, Russia, Madagascar, and the United States. A fully natural citrine is rare, and most citrine available in the market is heat-treated to enhance its color. Citrine is widely known as the "merchant's stone" as it is believed to bring prosperity and success.

Structure

The structure of citrine follows other varieties of quartz. It has a hexagonal crystal system and is commonly found in crystal clusters, geodes, and drusy. Citrine can be distinguished from other gemstones, such as amethyst, smoky quartz, and topaz, by its orange-to-brown color. Citrine is known for its unique lattice structure, which can help facilitate better concentration, enhance mental clarity, and promote inner peace.

Hardness

Citrine is a hard mineral and falls at seven on the Mohs scale of hardness, which means it is relatively tough and not easily breakable. However, despite its hardness, it is still scratchable by harder minerals such as diamond and corundum. Thus, keeping your citrine away from abrasive materials that can scratch or damage it is advisable.

Ways to Identify

Identifying citrine is relatively easy as the gemstone is distinct in color and structure. Due to its color and clarity, citrine is commonly mistaken for topaz or golden beryl. However, you can differentiate citrine from other gemstones by examining its structure and color. Topaz typically has a different crystal structure and is more transparent, whereas golden beryl is a lighter shade of yellow. Additionally, the presence of inclusions in citrine distinguishes it from other gemstones.

Uses

Apart from adorning jewelry, citrine is widely used in energy healing practices. Its healing properties include bringing positivity, boosting self-esteem, and promoting inner balance. Citrine can also be useful in feng shui practices to attract wealth and abundance into your life. If you're interested in meditation, citrine's energy can support achieving greater spiritual awareness.

In a nutshell, citrine is a beautiful gemstone with distinctive properties that separate it from other crystals. Whether you're a metaphysical enthusiast or a gemstone collector, owning a citrine can be a valuable addition to your collection. Remember to handle your citrine carefully and avoid exposing it to harsh conditions that can affect its beauty and properties. Overall, it's safe to say that citrine is a fantastic gemstone with much to offer, so add it to your collection today!

Quartz isn't just interesting because of its abundance or industrial uses. It has been valued for centuries for its beauty and metaphysical properties. Clear quartz, in particular, is believed to have healing properties and the ability to enhance mental clarity and focus. Rose quartz is used for promoting love and compassion, while amethyst is said to aid in spiritual growth and stress relief. These beliefs may not have scientific backing, but they certainly add to the allure of this fascinating mineral.

Quartz is a mineral that is both incredibly common and endlessly fascinating. The unique properties of quartz and its wide range of uses make it an important part of our everyday lives, whether we realize it or not. So next time you come across a quartz crystal or a piece of quartz jewelry, take a moment to appreciate the beauty and wonder of this amazing mineral.

Chapter 7: Chalcedonies and Agates

Agates and chalcedony are amazing stones that have been prized for centuries. Both of these classes of rocks are part of a greater family, the majestic quartz. Although agate and chalcedony are similar, each one has its unique charm and appeal. Agate is a beautiful, banded stone, often with captivating swirls or patterns. On the other hand, chalcedony is usually a solid color, ranging from an almost pastel pink to an intense dark blue. Despite having different characteristics, both of these stones are incredibly desirable.

Jewelers prize the durability and interesting features which they bring to accessories and artwork. With such stunning natural elements to work with, it's no wonder that people have enjoyed gems like agate and chalcedony for so long. This chapter will provide an introduction to the two stones, their properties, examples of both types, and tips on how to care for them. By the end, you'll be an expert on agate and chalcedony!

Introduction to Chalcedonies

Chalcedony is one of the most stunning gems in the world of jewelry. The gemstone comes in different variations of colors, including blue, white, gray, pink, and peach. It is popular for its various healing properties, which make it an excellent addition to any crystal healing regimen.

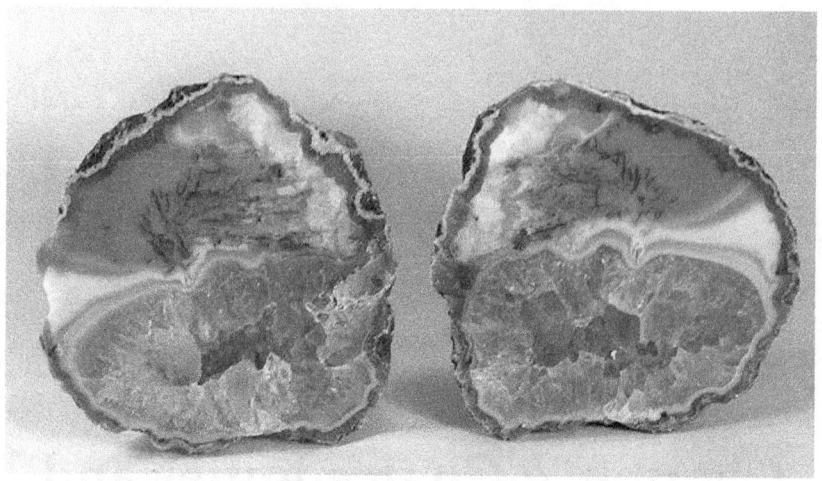

Chalcedony.
Rob Lavinsky, iRocks.com – CC-BY-SA-3.0, CC BY-SA 3.0
<https://creativecommons.org/licenses/by-sa/3.0>, via Wikimedia Commons
https://commons.wikimedia.org/wiki/File:Chalcedony-121273.jpg

What Is Chalcedony?

Chalcedony is a mineral that belongs to the quartz family and comprises microscopic crystals. It is generally found inside volcanic rocks, and its color variations depend on the minerals contained in the environment of its formation. This gemstone is considered one of the oldest minerals used for decorative purposes and has been a popular gemstone throughout history.

Properties of Chalcedony

1. **Color:** Chalcedony comes in various colors, including blue, white, gray, pink, and peach. Blue chalcedony is the most popular among them. It's a beautiful, serene, and calming color that helps bring peace and calmness to the wearer.
2. **Hardness and Durability:** Chalcedony has a hardness of six to seven on the Mohs scale, making it a relatively durable gemstone. It's essential to keep in mind that the gemstone can fracture easily, so it's important to handle it with care.
3. **Banding:** Banded chalcedony is a beautiful variation of the gemstone that comes with unique patterns and swirls. These patterns occur when the chalcedony forms next to another mineral, creating lines and swirls of color inside the stone.

4. **Healing Properties:** Chalcedony is known for its healing properties, making it an excellent choice for anyone seeking emotional balance, peace, and tranquility. This gemstone is believed to help overcome feelings of inferiority and bring out the inner strength and confidence of the wearer. Additionally, chalcedony is thought to provide physical benefits such as improving gut health and blood circulation.
5. **Metaphysical Properties:** In the world of spirituality, chalcedony is associated with the throat chakra, which governs communication and self-expression. This gemstone is believed to help the wearer speak their truth, improve their communication skills, and eliminate fear and anxiety associated with public speaking.

Types of Chalcedony

Chalcedony, with its beautiful and special characteristics, is truly one of the most fascinating minerals to ever exist. This type of mineral belongs to the quartz family and can come in various types. One of the most amazing characteristics of chalcedony is that it can form in a wide range of colors, each with unique properties. This section will explore some of the most popular types of chalcedony gems. From carnelian to onyx, we look forward to taking you on a journey to discover these wonderful types of chalcedony.

A. Carnelian

Carnelian is a gorgeous orange-to-reddish-brown mineral. It is a semi-precious stone and one of the most sought-after varieties of chalcedony. Its distinctive reddish-brown color is due to the presence of iron oxide within the mineral. Its properties include inner strength, courage, and creativity. When wearing carnelian, people can tap into their natural intuition and manifest their desires more easily. It is known to activate the second and third chakras, which enhance physical and mental vitality, renewed energy, increased creativity, and improved self-esteem.

B. Chrysoprase

Chrysoprase has a delicate green color that is reminiscent of fresh foliage in the spring season. It is known for its healing properties and is considered a powerful cleansing stone. Wearing chrysoprase can help you release negative thoughts and emotions while grounding your spiritual journey. The healing energy of chrysoprase can also recharge your energy field, attracting abundance, prosperity, and good luck.

C. Heliotrope

Heliotrope, also known as bloodstone, is a striking green mineral with streaks of red that can resemble a blood spatter. It is considered a powerful healing stone, believed to help purify the blood and relax the mind. It is also a popular stone for those trying to overcome emotional pains such as sadness, stress, and anxiety. Heliotrope can balance emotions and promote inner peace.

D. Chrome Chalcedony

One of the most unique varieties of chalcedony is chrome chalcedony. It has a stunning green color and can be transparent or translucent. Its properties include calming the mind while increasing intuition and emotional balance. When wearing it, one can feel their third eye chakra opening and their emotional center aligning with their spiritual journey. It can help release past emotional traumas and bring clarity and focus to the present.

E. Tiger's Eye

Tiger's eye is a rich golden-brown color with streaks of yellow and red. It is a powerful stone that can boost confidence and self-esteem and can help bring success to one's personal or professional life. Its properties include a mind-calming effect that balances negative emotions such as anxiety and insecurity. Tiger's eye is a practical stone that can help manifest the desired goals of those who wear it.

F. Jasper

Jasper can come in various colors, each with unique properties. It is considered a stabilizing stone that can help balance one's physical, emotional, and spiritual aspects. When wearing it, jasper carries nurturing energy that can promote comfort and security. It can help one release energy blocks, promoting positivity and drawing abundance to one's life.

G. Onyx

Onyx is a black mineral with a glossy finish. It represents strength, protection, and self-confidence. It is said to aid a person in controlling and focusing their energy while releasing negative emotions such as anxiety, depression, and anger. Wearing onyx can provide strength during mental or physical stress, making it a popular choice for those working in fast-paced or high-stress environments.

The different types of chalcedony are both beautiful and meaningful in their unique way. Each stone carries properties that can help enhance one's energy and well-being. Carnelian, chrysoprase, heliotrope, chrome chalcedony, tiger's eye, jasper, and onyx are just a few of the many types of chalcedony. Take the time to discover which one resonates with you and aids in your spiritual journey. Remember, chalcedony has something to offer everyone, making it a timeless and essential mineral to explore.

The Marvelous World of Agates

Agates are some of the most stunning, colorful, and intriguing crystals. You may have heard of them before, or maybe you haven't. But have you ever wondered what these rocks are and how they are formed? Well, this section will introduce you to the enchanting world of agates, from their basic properties to their intricate formations and how they are treasured by collectors, jewelry makers, and geology enthusiasts.

Agate.
James St. John, CC BY 2.0 <https://creativecommons.org/licenses/by/2.0>, via Wikimedia Commons https://commons.wikimedia.org/wiki/File:Agate_(Adrasman_City,_Tajikistan)_(32755918215).jpg

What Is an Agate?

Agates are a type of chalcedony mineral, which is composed of microcrystalline quartz formed from volcanic or sedimentary rocks. This mineral holds many secrets that give each agate its unique personality, ranging from striking bands of colors, subtle hues, or even translucent or opaque variations. The colorful and detailed designs in the rocks come from minerals like iron, manganese, and silica. These minerals enter the rock through tiny holes and cracks. The mix of these minerals creates a latticework of banding or other forms of inclusions that make each agate one-of-a-kind.

Properties of Agates

1. **Color:** Agates come in a wide spectrum of colors, ranging from fiery reds, oranges, and yellows to serene greens, blues, and purples, and subtle grays, whites, and browns. Some agates are solid in color, while others display intricate patterns that resemble landscapes, eyes, seascapes, and many more. Expert lapidaries and jewelers often use the color and patterns of agates to create stunning pieces that highlight the natural beauty of these stones.

2. **Hardness and Durability:** Agates are relatively hard minerals, with a rating of six-and-a-half to seven on the Mohs hardness scale. This makes them a popular choice for use in jewelry, decorative objects, and even sculptures due to their durability and resistance to scratches or chipping. They also have a high chemical corrosion resistance, making them ideal for use in chemical apparatus, such as test tubes, flasks, and mortars.

3. **Banding:** The banding of agates is one of the most distinctive features that make them so prized by collectors and enthusiasts. Banding is a series of alternating layers of minerals that create a wavy or straight-line pattern that runs across the agate. The patterns can be asymmetrical, symmetrical, or radial, often resembling natural landscapes, waves, or other natural phenomena. Sometimes smaller inclusions like an "eye" or "bloat" (where gas bubbles were trapped during the formation of the agate) break up the banding in some places.

4. **Varieties:** There are many types of agates, each with its own properties, colors, and patterns. Some of the most popular types of agates include fire agate which displays a brilliant range of orange and red hues; blue lace agate, known for its delicate blue to white lacy pattern; and Botswana, featuring a distinct grey to darker gray banding. Other notable types of agates include crazy lace and landscape. Plume agates are also stunning and coveted by collectors and enthusiasts alike.

Types of Agate

If you are a gemstone lover or a believer in the healing properties of crystals, you may already be familiar with the mystical agate. This unique mineral is widely popular for its rich colors, intricate patterns, and metaphysical properties. But did you know that agate also comes in various types that exhibit distinct features and meanings?

A. Blue Lace Agate

Blue lace agate is a stunning variety of agate characterized by its delicate blue and white striped pattern. This crystal is revered for its calming and uplifting energy, which helps to soothe stress, anxiety, and emotional turmoil. Blue lace agate is also believed to enhance communication, clarity, and creativity, making it an ideal stone for artists, writers, and speakers. This crystal is often used in meditation, spiritual healing, and chakra balancing, as it can help to calm the mind and promote inner peace.

B. Fire Agate

Fire agate is a mesmerizing variety of agate that displays a rainbow-like iridescence and a fiery glow. This crystal is known for its grounding and protective properties, which help to stabilize energy, foster courage, and ward off negative energies. Fire agate is also regarded as a creativity and manifestation stone that can help to amplify one's desires and manifest their dreams into reality. This crystal is popular among jewelers and crystal collectors due to its unique appearance and powerful energy.

C. Moss Agate

Moss agate is a distinctive variety of agate with beautiful green moss-like patterns on its surface. This crystal is highly regarded for its connection to nature and its ability to promote growth, abundance, and harmony. Moss agate is believed to facilitate communication with plants and animals, as it is said to embody the spirit of the natural world. This crystal is popular among gardeners, environmentalists, and outdoor enthusiasts seeking to align with the Earth's energy and promote ecological balance.

D. Dendritic Agate

Dendritic agate is a captivating variety of agates with unique brown or black dendritic inclusions resembling ferns, trees, or other organic forms. This crystal symbolizes growth, stability, and balance, as it embodies the essence of nature's creative power. Dendritic agate is often used for enhancing visualization, intuition, and connection with the natural world. This crystal is ideal for nature lovers, healers, and environmentalists who seek to promote personal and planetary healing.

Agates vs. Chalcedonies: What Makes Them Different?

Agates and chalcedonies can easily be mistaken for each other. Both are stunningly beautiful and come in breathtaking colors, but what exactly sets them apart? Understanding the difference between these two gems can help you choose the perfect one for your collection.

Differences in Structure

One of the main differences between agates and chalcedonies is their internal structure. Agates have a distinctive banding pattern that is caused by the deposition of minerals in layers or rings around the walls of the hollow cavity where the stone formed. Chalcedonies, on the other hand, do not have this banding pattern, but they often have microcrystalline structures that create a waxy surface.

Color Variations

Agates and chalcedonies come in a wide range of colors, but each stone's colors and patterns differ. Agates have distinct patterns, including eye-shaped markings, stripes, and concentric rings that come in different colors, ranging from earthy browns and greens to vibrant reds, blues, and purples. On the other hand, chalcedonies are usually solid in color, with light blue, gray, and white being the most common colors.

Different Uses

Agates are often used for beads, tumbled stones, and cabochon cut gems because of their distinctive bands of colors. They are also used for decorative items such as bookends, coasters, and vases. Chalcedonies are often used for carvings, cameos, and intaglios because of their dense structure and waxy luster. They are also used for beads, pendants, and other jewelry pieces.

Caring for Chalcedonies and Agates

Taking care of chalcedonies and agates is both simple and rewarding. The most important part of caring for these beautiful stones is keeping them clean to help maintain their stunning colors and unique patterns. Cleaning with a soft, damp cloth is the safest way, as harsh detergents can damage them. Avoid using any type of chemical exposure, such as cleaning solutions or steam cleaners, when caring for your collection. When storing them, ensure they are kept in a cool, dry place away from direct sunlight to protect the beauty of these precious stones. Anytime you wear jewelry containing agates or chalcedonies, be sure to remove it before participating in activities that may be too strenuous for the delicate metals used in settings. Following these few steps is all it takes for these gems, which boast incredible variety in their color pallets and luster, to last for many years.

Chalcedony is a stunning gemstone that is rich in beauty and healing power. Whether you're seeking emotional balance, personal strength, or a way to improve your overall well-being, there is much to gain from this gemstone. With so many variations and benefits, it's no wonder that chalcedonies have remained a popular choice among jewelry enthusiasts throughout history. So, if you're looking for a gemstone that is as beautiful as it is beneficial, chalcedony is undoubtedly the perfect choice for you.

Agate is a fascinating mineral that has a wide variety of patterns, colors, and metaphysical properties. Whether you are drawn to the calming energy of Blue lace agate, the protective energy of fire agate, the harmonizing energy of moss agate, or the growth-oriented energy of dendritic agate, there is an agate variety that can suit your needs and enhance your life. So, next time you come across an agate stone or a piece of agate jewelry, take a closer look and try to discover its type and meaning. Who knows, you may just find the perfect crystal to support your spiritual journey and personal growth.

Chapter 8: Precious Gemstones

Precious gemstones have been treasured since antiquity and are admired for their dazzling colors as well as their rarity. Over the centuries, these gems have been a status symbol, exchanged as gifts of love or worn to bring good luck. Whether you appreciate the beauty of a deep sapphire blue, a joyful yellow topaz, or an elegant pink diamond, there is something timeless and magical about gemstones that continues to captivate us today. Their luxurious allure makes them desirable items that are worthy investments in any jewelry collection.

This chapter will discuss the four precious gemstones. It will cover their characteristics, how to identify them, as well as mining and polishing techniques. Lastly, it will explain what makes these stones so precious in the first place. By this chapter's end, you will better understand these rare and valuable gems.

Precious Gemstones: The Shimmering World of Elegance

Gemstones have been a part of human civilization for centuries. From royalty to commoners, everyone has been fascinated by precious gemstones. These colorful, sparkling, finest examples of Mother Nature symbolize elegance, luxury, and status. Each precious gemstone has its beauty, origin, and cultural significance.

Origins of Gemstones

Gemstones are formed deep inside the Earth, under extreme pressure and heat over millions of years. Each precious gemstone has a unique origin story. For example, emeralds are formed in the metamorphic rocks of Colombia, while sapphires originate from Sri Lanka's alluvial deposits. The rarity and origin of gemstones determine their value.

Classification of Gemstones

Gemstones are categorized based on their chemical composition and optical properties. The four categories of precious stones are diamonds, emeralds, rubies, and sapphires. While other gemstones like turquoise, amethyst, and garnet are considered semi-precious, they hold significant value in the jewelry industry.

Significance of Gemstones

Gemstones have cultural significance and are considered an expression of one's personality. For example, sapphires are considered a symbol of wisdom, loyalty, and truth. Similarly, rubies represent courage and passion, emeralds represent fertility and prosperity, and diamonds symbolize love and commitment. Gemstones are also associated with astrological properties and are believed to have healing powers.

Price of Gemstones

The cost of a gemstone depends on several factors, like how rare it is, its quality, how big it is, and where it comes from. Diamonds are the most expensive and valuable gemstones, followed by emeralds, sapphires, and rubies. The quality of a gemstone is judged based on the four Cs- cut, clarity, carat, and color.

Caring for Gemstones

Gemstones are delicate and require proper care to maintain their luster and value. Exposure to heat, chemicals, or rough handling can damage them. It is crucial to store them in a cool, dry place and avoid wearing them during strenuous activities like exercise, swimming, or gardening. Regular cleaning and maintenance are essential to keep the gemstones looking their best.

Emeralds: The Gemstone of Royalty

Emeralds have been known to be one of the most exquisite and sought-after gemstones for centuries. The vibrancy of their green color pays homage to life, nature, and growth. Wearing an emerald gemstone can bring the wearer happiness, peace, and prosperity. This section will discuss the characteristics and identification of emeralds so you can understand and appreciate the value and luxury of owning them.

Characteristics

Emeralds belong to the beryl family of minerals and are characterized by their vivid green color, transparency, and luster. The color of emeralds is due to the presence of chromium ions in them. These stones may have visible inclusions called "jardin," French for *garden*, and can be seen as moss-like formations inside the gem. The inclusions do not necessarily diminish the beauty of the emerald, as they may enhance its unique character.

Identification

Identifying an emerald gemstone requires a bit of experience and technical knowledge. Below are some common ways to identify an emerald stone:

1. **Color:** Emeralds are known for their distinct green color. However, it is not merely green, so make sure to look for their tone, saturation, and hues. The most sought-after color is an intense green with hints of blue.
2. **Clarity:** Inclusions are typical in emeralds, but make sure they are not too prominent to be seen with the naked eye. Professionals can use magnification tools to observe the gemstone's clarity.
3. **Cut:** Emeralds are delicate, so they should be cut to enhance the stone's natural beauty. The emerald cut is the most common, which reveals the stone's clarity and establishes a distinct yet elegant appeal.
4. **Carat:** An emerald is measured in carats, with good quality, and a smaller emerald is worth more than a larger and inferior quality stone. Consider carat weight, color, clarity, and cut when purchasing an emerald.

Emeralds have long been admired by royalty and are still considered to be one of the most valuable gemstones. The beauty, rarity, and significance of this gemstone are undeniable. If you intend to purchase an emerald, exercise caution and seek professional guidance to ensure the stone's authenticity. Owning an emerald enhances the aura and brings the wearer happiness, peace, and prosperity.

Diamonds

Diamonds have symbolized love and devotion for centuries – and it's easy to see why. Their dazzling sparkle, durability, and rarity make them one of the most sought-after gemstones in the world. But what exactly makes a diamond so special? Let's explore the characteristics and identification of diamonds, so you can learn everything you need to know about these stunning gemstones.

Characteristics of Diamonds

Diamonds are created in the Earth's mantle under extreme pressure and heat and are made of a single element: carbon. They are the hardest naturally occurring substance on Earth, so they are highly resistant to scratching and breaking. Additionally, diamonds have a unique ability to refract light, giving them their signature sparkle and fire.

How to Identify a Diamon

There are a few crucial characteristics to search for while identifying diamonds. The "four Cs" — carat weight, cut, color, and clarity — come first. "Carat weight" refers to the diamond's weight, with one carat equaling 0.2 grams. The term "cut" describes how the diamond has been fashioned, and it significantly impacts the diamond's worth and brilliance. The diamond's color describes how colorless or yellow it appears, with perfectly colorless diamonds being the most expensive. The presence of imperfections or flaws within the diamond is called *clarity;* fewer inclusions results in greater value.

In addition to the four Cs, there are a few other ways to identify diamonds. One is using a loupe, a specialized magnifying glass that lets you see the diamond up close. You can also use a diamond tester, which uses thermal conductivity to test if a gemstone is a real diamond. However, the best way to ensure you're getting a real diamond is to purchase it from a reputable jeweler who has certified the diamond's authenticity.

Not all diamonds are created equal. Some diamonds are treated with high heat or radiation to enhance their color or clarity, which can impact their value. Also, diamonds can be ethically sourced or come from conflict zones, so it's critical to research and purchase from a jeweler who sources their diamonds responsibly.

Diamonds are truly special gemstones with unique characteristics and rich history. Understanding the four Cs and other identification methods can help ensure that you're getting a high-quality diamond. And when purchasing a diamond, always choose a reputable jeweler who sources them ethically. With this knowledge, you're ready to explore the world of diamonds and find the perfect piece of jewelry to treasure for years to come.

Rubies

Rubies are one of the most sought-after gemstones in the world. A gemstone that is fiery, passionate, and captivating in every possible way. Rubies have been prized for their vibrant color, rarity, and history for thousands of years. From royals to commoners, rubies have always been revered and sought after.

Characteristics

Rubies are most well-known for their striking red color. But not all rubies are created equal. Rubies can vary in color from deep red to pinkish-red and even purple-red tones. The color of rubies is caused by the presence of chromium within the crystal structure. The more chromium, the deeper and richer the red color of the ruby.

Identifying Rubies

Rubies are one of the hardest gemstones and are also very durable. They rank nine on the Mohs hardness scale, indicating their superior toughness. This makes rubies perfect for everyday wear jewelry, including engagement rings or other frequently worn pieces. Rubies are usually found in metamorphic rocks but may also be found in sedimentary rocks or igneous.

Significance

Did you know that rubies have a rich history? The first recorded ruby dates back to ancient India, where they were used as talismans to ward off evil spirits. Today, they are still considered a symbol of love and passion and are often gifted for romantic occasions such as anniversaries, Valentine's Day, or engagement presents. Additionally, rubies have been associated with prosperity, peace, and power throughout history.

Rubies are also incredibly rare, and their scarcity is another reason for their high value. The most significant supply now comes from Burma, Sri Lanka, and Thailand. However, it is important to note that not all rubies are natural. Many are now created in laboratories, and it can be difficult to distinguish between natural and lab-created rubies. Synthetic ruby is made to be the same as natural ruby and has excellent clarity, which is why some people prefer them over natural rubies because it is not as expensive.

Sapphires: The Timeless Beauty

When it comes to precious stones, sapphires are among the favorites. Known for their stunning beauty and durability, sapphires are popular for engagement rings, anniversary gifts, and other special occasions. But what exactly are sapphires, and what makes them so special? This section will take a closer look at sapphires, including their characteristics and how to identify them correctly.

Characteristics

Sapphires are a type of corundum mineral that is second only to diamonds in terms of hardness. They come in various colors, but the most well-known color is blue. Sapphires are often synonymous with blue, but they can come in other colors like pink, yellow, orange, green, and even white. The color of sapphire is caused by different impurities or the presence of specific minerals, such as iron or titanium.

Identifying Sapphires

One thing that makes sapphires unique is their ability to change color depending on the lighting conditions. A sapphire that looks blue under natural light can appear purple or violet in incandescent light. This phenomenon is called pleochroism, and it is a characteristic that is only present in certain gemstones, such as sapphires. Another way to identify a sapphire is by its luster, which is the way it reflects light. Sapphires have a brilliant or vitreous luster, which means that they shine brightly under the light. However, this is not unique to sapphires, as many other minerals have similar luster.

The most effective way to distinguish a sapphire is through its clarity and its cut. High-quality sapphires have excellent clarity, free from any inclusions or blemishes that can affect their sparkle and shine. The cut of sapphire can also affect its overall beauty, as it can enhance or diminish the stone's color and brilliance. The carat weight of a sapphire does not necessarily dictate its value, as other factors like color, clarity, and cut play essential roles in determining its worth. However, sapphires that are larger than four carats are rare and can command a high price.

Sapphires are truly timeless and remain a favorite among gemstone enthusiasts. Their unique characteristics, including their stunning colors, pleochroism, luster, clarity, and cut, make them a popular choice for jewelry making. Whether in the market for an engagement ring or a special gift, sapphires are always an excellent option. Remember, when purchasing a sapphire, always check for its color, clarity, cut, and luster to ensure that you're getting value for your money.

Mining, Cutting, and Polishing

Precious gemstones are fascinating and hold a special place in everyone's hearts. We have used these stunning gems for jewelry, decor, and even medicinal purposes for centuries. But have you ever wondered how these gems are sourced, cut, and polished to make them so dazzling?

Mining

Gemstones are found in various places worldwide. They can be excavated from the earth, mined from underwater beds, and even found in meteorites.

There are four methods of mining gemstones:

- Alluvial mining
- Open-pit mining
- Seabed mining
- Underground mining

Open-pit mining is used to access shallow deposits of gemstones that can be easily extracted. Alluvial mining involves extracting semi-precious stones from sediment deposited on riverbeds. Underground mining is when gems are extracted from deep under the Earth's surface. Lastly, seabed mining is used to extract gems from ocean sediments.

Cutting

Once the gemstones have been extracted, they are sent to a cutting facility. Here, skilled artisans use various tools to shape the gemstones into desired shapes and sizes. The most common tools used for cutting gemstones include saws, grinding wheels, and polishing wheels. It takes years of training and experience to become a skilled gemstone cutter.

Polishing

Once the gems have been cut, they are handed over to the polishers. The goal of polishing is to give the gemstones a mirror-like finish. Polishers use a series of abrasive materials, such as diamond powder, to remove the scratches and create a smooth surface on the gemstone.

Finally, the polishing wheel is used to create the final mirror finish on the gemstone.

The Importance of Ethical Sourcing

With the growing concern about unethical mining practices, we must ensure that the gemstones we buy are ethically sourced. The Kimberley Process Certification Scheme (KPCS) is an international certification scheme that ensures that rough diamonds are mined, cut, and exported ethically. Furthermore, many gemstone companies have joined hands to create responsible sourcing initiatives that address environmental and social issues.

Mining, cutting, and polishing precious gemstones is an arduous process but one that produces beautiful and timeless gems. It takes an experienced team of miners, cutters, and polishers to create the perfect gemstone. Knowing about ethical sourcing is crucial to ensure that the gemstones we buy are conflict-free. The world of precious gemstones is fascinating, and understanding the process of mining, cutting, and polishing makes us appreciate these beautiful gems all the more.

Gemstones are a mesmerizing creation of nature that has been admired and treasured throughout history. Their beauty, rarity, and cultural significance make them valuable and cherished possessions. From birthstones to engagement rings, gemstones have a special place in our hearts and have become an integral part of the jewelry industry. However, their value extends beyond their monetary worth, as they remind us of our emotions, beliefs, and aspirations. So, the next time you admire a sparkling gemstone, remember that it is not just a piece of jewelry but a symbol of elegance, luxury, and individuality.

Chapter 9: Semi-Precious Gemstones

Semi-precious gemstones are some of Earth's rarest and most beautiful items, often found in gorgeous blues, pinks, purples, and more. Semi-precious stones offer an intriguing insight into the world of geology, with each stone one-of-a-kind in its composition and shape. Not only do semi-precious gemstones make striking pieces to be used for jewelry, but they also introduce a wonderful element of luxury and class to any space. Used as part of home decor, these stones can add an air of subtle sophistication that is truly something special.

This chapter will cover the different types of semi-precious gemstones. It'll dive into the different gemstone families, from quartz to turquoise, and explain their characteristics, structure, and identification. Images of the different stones in each family will be included so you can get an up-close and personal look at their beauty. By the end of this chapter, you'll better understand the different semi-precious gemstones and be able to distinguish them from one another.

Overview of Semi-Precious Gemstones

There's something about gemstones that has always captured our fascination. Few things come close to the allure of these shimmering, iridescent natural gems that never seem to lose their charm. Amongst these jewels are semi-precious stones, often underrated but no less beautiful. Although they might lack the heart-stopping price tags of precious gemstones, they are nothing short of splendorous!

What Are Semi-Precious Gemstones?

Semi-precious stones are natural gemstones that don't fall into the "precious" category, which comprises diamonds, emeralds, rubies, and sapphires. These stones are also called colloquial "gemstones" or "semi-precious gems." However, they can be just as gorgeous, sparkling, and valuable as their precious counterparts. The market for semi-precious stones is vast and varied, so there's a huge range of stones to choose from at all price points.

Types of Semi-Precious Gemstones

Unlike precious stones, limited to a select few, semi-precious stones offer a wide range of colors and varieties. Most semi-precious stones come from mineral deposits in the Earth's crust, while others are organic or man-made. The variety of semiprecious stones is staggering, from aquamarine, amethyst, topaz, and jade to tourmaline, citrine, garnet, and many more!

Symbolism and Meaning of Semi-Precious Gemstones

Throughout history, semi-precious gemstones have acquired symbolic and mystical meanings and properties associated with them. These meanings tend to be based on spiritual, cultural, and personal beliefs. For instance, the garnet symbolizes peace and prosperity, while the amethyst is thought to offer protection against negative influences. Other stones carry more specific symbolism, such as rose quartz, which represents love, and moonstone, which is thought to bring good luck.

How to Care for Semi-Precious Gemstones?

As with precious stones, taking care of your semi-precious gems is important to preserve their beauty for years to come. While some of these stones are sturdy and can withstand daily wear, others are more delicate and require proper care. Here are some tips to ensure that you're taking good care of your gemstones:

- Handle gemstones with a clean cloth or gloves to prevent oil from your fingers from sticking to their surface
- Store them separately in their pouches or lined boxes to avoid scratches or damage from other jewelry
- Avoid exposing them to intense heat or sunlight
- Avoid subjecting them to harsh chemicals or cleaning agents

Semi-precious gemstones are a vibrant and fascinating world unto their own. They carry a plethora of symbolism and are available in so many varieties that it's impossible to pick just one favorite. So, whether you're a seasoned collector or a newbie on the hunt for your first piece of gemstone jewelry, consider the many possibilities semi-precious stones offer. Simply put, the splendor of these gems is your own to explore and enjoy.

Beryl Family Gemstones

If you're a fan of gemstones, you might have already heard about the beautiful and exotic beryl family of gemstones. Ranging from colors like yellow, green, blue, pink, and white, these gemstones are famous for their unique properties and characteristics. If you want to know more about the beryl family gemstones, their characteristics, structure, and how to identify them, read on to explore fascinating information about them and why they are ideal jewelry pieces.

Characteristics

Beryl is a mineral family consisting of several varieties of gemstones. While the most famous beryl gemstone is emerald, other gemstones, including aquamarine, morganite, heliodor, and goshenite, are also known to belong to the beryl family. The physical and chemical properties of beryl gemstones vary, with properties such as hardness, color, clarity, and transparency depending on the variety of beryl. For instance, while emerald belongs to the beryl family and typically exhibits a green color caused by the presence of chromium or vanadium, beryl gemstones like aquamarine have a distinct blue color.

Structure

In terms of structure, beryl family gemstones are hexagonal crystals composed mainly of beryllium aluminum silicate. They are characterized by their high refractive index of more than one-and-a-half and their ability to split light into two as it enters the crystal. These properties give beryl family gemstones a sparkling and bright appearance, making them an ideal choice for designers looking for radiant and vivid jewelry pieces. Moreover, beryl gemstones are known for their excellent toughness and resistance to scratches, making them perfect for everyday jewelry wear.

Identification

Identifying beryl family gemstones typically involves using a standard gemology testing process. Typically, gemstones' hardness and chemical and physical properties are used to identify them accurately. Beryl gemstones typically have a hardness rating of seven-and-a-half to eight, meaning they are hard to scratch. Depending on the gemstone variety, you can also identify beryl family gemstones through their characteristic color, which varies from deep green to light yellow or pink. Additionally, beryl gemstones have a distinctive crystal structure that makes them stand out from other minerals.

Uses

When it comes to jewelry, beryl family gemstones provide an excellent option for creating unique pieces that are both beautiful and durable. From rings, necklaces, and bracelets, beryl gemstones come in different colors and shades that can complement any outfit or skin tone. Whether you prefer a classic emerald cut emerald or a contemporary cushion cut morganite, beryl family gems are perfect for creating jewelry that tells a story and makes a statement.

Corundum Family Gemstones

As a gemstone enthusiast, you might have encountered the term "corundum family." But do you know what it means, its characteristics, and how to identify the different types? Corundum family gemstones are a group of minerals that belong to the oxide family, and their distinguishing feature is their high hardness. The hardness of corundum ranges between nine and 10 on the Mohs scale; the only mineral that is harder than corundum is diamond. Some of the most famous gemstones in the corundum family are sapphires and rubies, which are widely sought after for their stunning colors, durability, and rarity.

Structure

The corundum's structure is hexagonal, and its crystal pattern is usually flat and tabular. Corundum's color typically ranges from transparent to opaque; in some cases, it may contain small inclusions or surface blemishes. The color of corundum is mainly determined by small amounts of impurities in the crystal lattice. For instance, red corundum, the most valuable variety of corundum, is caused by the presence of chromium.

Identification

Identifying corundum family gemstones can be a bit tricky, particularly when they are not faceted. You can use several factors to identify corundum, including its hardness, density, and color. One of the most straightforward methods of identifying corundum is to use a refractometer that measures the light's refractive index as it moves through the gemstone. Due to the unique crystal structure, each gemstone has its distinctive refractive index, which can be used to identify its type.

Another critical characteristic of corundum family gemstones is their pleochroism, which means that it exhibits different colors when viewed from different angles. This trait is particularly noticeable in sapphires, which may appear blue from one angle, but purple from another. Rubies also exhibit a similar phenomenon but tend to show red to pinkish-red hues from most angles.

Tourmaline Family Gemstones

Tourmaline is a fascinating gemstone that comes in an array of colors and is known for its unique properties. Its crystal structure makes it a complex mineral species that has become popular in jewelry making. But, with so many colors and varieties, it can be challenging to differentiate between them.

Characteristics

The tourmaline family comprises 12 different mineral species ranging in color from black to pink, green, blue, yellow, and even bi-color or tri-color. Due to tourmaline's pleochroism, the color can vary based on the viewing angle. One of the most prized varieties is the Paraiba tourmaline, discovered in Brazil in the 1980s and had a unique, vivid blue-green color. Tourmaline is also known for displaying electric properties, creating pyroelectricity and piezoelectricity. This unique feature means that when you rub a tourmaline, it becomes electrically charged and can attract dust or even small pieces of paper.

Structure

The crystal structure of tourmaline is quite interesting, as it is classified as a cyclosilicate mineral. This means that the crystal structure is composed of rings of SiO_4 tetrahedrons. Each tourmaline crystal is a long, thin, three-sided prism with grooves and bumps along the sides. Mineral inclusions and the presence of other chemical elements can alter the shape of these prisms, resulting in a unique appearance for each tourmaline.

Identification

When it comes to identifying tourmaline, it can be quite challenging, as each species can have different physical and chemical characteristics. One of the most helpful tools in identifying tourmaline is its heightening color characteristics which can reveal the presence of specific elements. In addition, using a polariscope can help distinguish between different types of tourmaline, as some may show birefringence or even color zoning.

Another noteworthy aspect of tourmaline is its use in alternative medicine. This gemstone is believed to possess various healing properties, including mental clarity, anxiety relief, and energy balance. It is thought to help release negative ions and absorb electromagnetic radiation from electronic devices. Many people wear tourmaline jewelry during meditation or place tourmaline under their pillow to promote peaceful sleep.

Spinel Family Gemstones

These gemstones are often overlooked, but they hold an unmatched beauty equal to that of any other gemstone family and are just waiting to be discovered.

Characteristics

Spinel family gemstones are mineral-based, and they belong to a group of gemstones that are made up of various elements. These gemstones can be found in many colors, such as blue, green, pink, and yellow. Spinel gemstones are known for their durability and hardness, which ranges from seven-and-a-half to eight on the Mohs scale. The spinel family of gemstones comprises magnesium aluminate, a mineral that forms crystals in a cubic system.

Structure

Spinel family gemstones feature unique structures, which makes them different from other gemstones. The crystal structure of Spinel gemstones consists of a series of octahedral octets meaning that there are eight ions in each octahedron. This structure makes the gemstones denser and more robust than many other types. Spinel family gemstones also contain high amounts of chromium, which contributes to the gemstones' coloration.

Identification

Now that we know the spinel family's structure and what comprises them, let's look at how to identify them. It can be challenging to identify spinel gemstones, as they often get mistaken for other gemstones, such as ruby or sapphire. However, a few unique features distinguish spinel gemstones from other gemstones. One such feature is their single refraction, differentiating them from double-refracting gemstone types. Spinel gemstones also register twinned or interpenetrating spinel crystals, which is a characteristic that is unique to them.

In addition to their unique features, spinel family gemstones have a fascinating history. The gemstones were named after the Latin word *spina*, meaning "thorn." During ancient times, spinel gemstones were believed to have properties such as healing illness and protecting their wearer from harm. The gemstones also played a significant role in many royal jewelry pieces throughout history, such as being a centerpiece gemstone in the British crown jewels.

Other Semi-Precious Gemstones

The world is full of beautiful gemstones that never cease to amaze us with their exquisite beauty and unique characteristics. Amongst the most beautiful and enigmatic of them are the garnet, opal, turquoise, and peridot. These gemstones have a rich history, and their popularity in jewelry continues to skyrocket steadily. Here are some more details about each of these precious gems.

Garnet Family Gemstones

The garnet comes in a variety of colors, including red, green, and yellow. This gemstone is a silicate mineral with six variants: grossular, spessartine, andradite, uvarovite, pyrope, and almandine. These variations give garnets different chemical compositions and, therefore, different hues. Garnets are easily identified by their crystal structure and are usually found in the metamorphic rocks of the Earth's crust. Additionally, it is not easily scratched, making it a perfect choice for jewelry.

Opal Family Gemstones

Opals come in different colors ranging from white to black. Most opals have a rainbow-like play of colors, making them highly sought after in the jewelry world. These gemstones are formed from silica gel that seeps into cracks and crevices of rocks, hardening over time. Opals are not durable gemstones, and that's because they contain a lot of water, making them more prone to cracking and chipping. To identify an opal, look for the unique play of colors and its pearly luster.

Turquoise Family Gemstones

Turquoise is a blue-green gemstone that is highly valued for its mid-blue color. It is a relatively soft gemstone, ranking just below quartz on the Mohs hardness scale. Turquoise occurs in arid regions and is often found in association with copper deposits. The gemstone has a granular structure and is easily identifiable by its waxy luster.

Peridot Family Gemstones

Peridot is a green gemstone with a yellowish-green color. It is a mineral found in ultramafic rocks such as peridotite and meteorites. Peridot is relatively hard, ranking six-and-a-half to seven on the Mohs scale of hardness. It is easily identified by its high refraction index and double refraction.

Garnet, opal, turquoise, and peridot gemstones are a representation of the Earth's beauty and diversity. Each gemstone has unique features that make it stand out in the jewelry world. While garnets are known for their rich colors and exquisite beauty, opals are loved for their unique play of colors. Turquoises are valued for their unique blue-green color, and peridots for their yellow-green color. Whether you're a lover of gemstones or just getting started on collecting them, these gemstones should make it to your list.

Semi-precious gemstones are some of the most sought-after gemstones in the jewelry world. Each gemstone has unique characteristics that make them stand out from each other and make them all the more special. Whether you're looking for a piece of jewelry with a pop of color or something classic and timeless, these gemstones will surely be the perfect addition to your collection. With their beauty, durability, and unique characteristics, these gemstones will bring a sparkle of joy to you and your loved ones. So, don't hesitate to add these beautiful semi-precious gems to your collection today!

Chapter 10: Meteorites and Tektites

Meteorites and tektites are two amazing space features that fascinate the modern world. Meteorites are comprised of pieces of rock or metal that have traveled from space and landed on Earth's surface. Conversely, Tektites are generally rounded rocks and pebbles created when meteorites impacted Earth's surface and melted part of the planet's crust. The individual elements found in these two types of cosmic occurrences allow scientists to better understand how our universe operates.

Understanding more about meteorites and tektites opens up a unique window into an unseen world and is truly an exciting prospect for those seeking further knowledge about our time in the cosmos. This chapter will focus on the definition of meteorites and tektites, the various types of each, and ways to identify them. Examples of well-known specimens of meteorites and tektites will also be discussed. By the end of this chapter, you will be more familiar with the fascinating world of meteorites and tektites.

Definition of Meteorites and Tektites

Meteorites and tektites are two components of *meteoritics*, the study of objects that originate from space. Meteorites are pieces of solid material that have fallen to Earth from outer space, typically formed when an asteroid or comet enters the atmosphere. Tektites are glassy objects found on Earth that, it is speculated, have resulted from the impact between Earth and extraterrestrial objects. While meteorites come in various sizes and forms, ranging from small stones to large chunks of rock, tektites are generally dark greenish or brownish with a glossy appearance. Both meteorites and tektites are valuable sources of knowledge. Studying them can give us insight into the origin of our solar system and help scientists understand the impact of collisions between asteroids in space.

Types of Meteorites

Meteorites have been recorded since ancient times. These solid pieces of debris from outer space have traveled across the vast expanse of our universe before finally ending up on our planet. The study of meteorites has given us valuable information into the formation and evolution of our solar system.

Meteorite.
Doug Bowman from DeKalb IL, USA, CC BY 2.0
<*https://creativecommons.org/licenses/by/2.0*>, *via Wikimedia Commons*
https://commons.wikimedia.org/wiki/File:Oriented_Meteorite.jpg

A. Iron Meteorites

Iron meteorites are the easiest to recognize among the three types. These are made up of over 90% iron-nickel alloy and have a distinctive metallic appearance. They are believed to have formed in the core of a planetesimal, a small protoplanet formed from dust and gas in the early stages of the solar system. Iron meteorites are rich in minerals such as kamacite and taenite, which are responsible for the Widmanstätten patterns that can be observed when slicing a polished iron meteorite. These patterns are unique to iron meteorites and can be used to determine their origin.

B. Stony-Iron Meteorites

Stony-iron meteorites, also known as pallasites, are a combination of both iron and silicate minerals. They are believed to have formed at the boundary between the core and the mantle of a planetesimal. The silicate minerals in stony-iron meteorites are usually olivine and pyroxene and are located in the metal matrix, which gives the meteorites their unique appearance. Pallasites are one of the rarest types of meteorites, accounting for less than one percent of all known meteorites.

C. Stony Meteorites

Stony meteorites are the most abundant of the three types, accounting for over 90% of all meteorites ever found. They comprise silicate minerals such as olivine and pyroxene, similar to those found in the Earth's mantle. Stony meteorites can be further classified into two groups: chondrites and achondrites. Chondrites are the most primitive meteorites and are believed to be remnants from the early stages of the solar system. On the other hand, Achondrites have undergone some degree of differentiation, meaning they have experienced some form of geological processing.

Types of Tektites

Tektites are unique, beautiful, and visually stunning. But have you ever wondered about their origin or types? Tektites are formed when a meteor strikes the Earth's surface, and the impact causes a pressure wave that melts the surrounding rocks. This molten material then cools and solidifies into a glassy structure commonly referred to as a tektite.

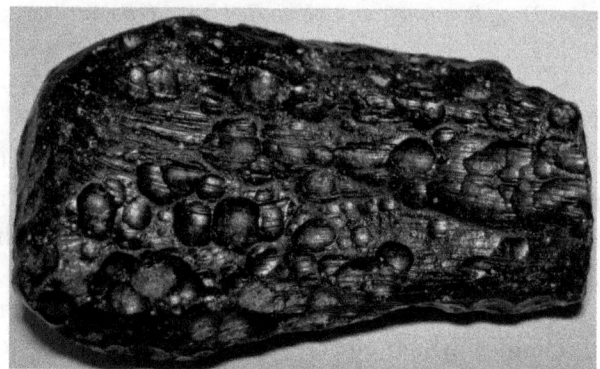

27. Tektite.

James St. John, CC BY 2.0 <https://creativecommons.org/licenses/by/2.0>, via Wikimedia Commons https://commons.wikimedia.org/wiki/File:Indochinite_tektite_(Pleistocene,_783-803_ka;_Australasian_Tektite_Strewn_Field,_southeastern_Asia)_6.jpg

1. Microtektites

This type of tektite is incredibly small, typically measuring less than one millimeter across. Microtektites are created when a meteor impact occurs and sends tiny glass fragments into the atmosphere. Microtektites do not originate from the melting of rocks or other materials on the Earth's surface. This type of tektite can float in the atmosphere for a long time, creating a phenomenon called tektite rain. It also reminds us of the catastrophic events that have occurred in our planet's history.

2. Muong-Nong Type Tektites

This type of tektite was first discovered in Vietnam in 1938. It is primarily found in Indochina, Cambodia, and Laos. The muong-nong-type tektites are dark brown or black and shaped like irregular droplets. They are about ten times heavier than a typical meteorite and comprise various elements like aluminum, silicon, magnesium, and more. Scientists believe that the muong-nong type tektites might be one of the oldest forms of tektites that exist on our planet.

3. Splash-Form Tektites

These tektites are the most abundant form across the planet. The splash-form tektites are formed when a meteorite strikes the Earth with such force that molten glass is created from the melting of rocks on the ground. The type of splash-form tektite found worldwide is based on the location of the meteorite impact. For example, Ivory Coast tektites are found in West Africa, while the North American tektites can be found around the Great Lakes region.

4. Australites

The australite tektites are unique because they were formed by multiple meteor impacts that hit several locations in southern Asia and around Australia. The australite tektites have a sleek, aerodynamic shape which is quite different from the other types of tektites. They are typically dark green, black, or brown and are found strewn in fields in Australia and Laos.

Famous Specimens of Meteorites and Tektites

- The night sky has always fascinated humans, and we have always been captivated by the amazing things that fall from it. One such thing is meteorites, which are pieces of asteroids or comets that reach the Earth's surface. Tektites, on the other hand, form from impact events on Earth, resulting in glassy rocks that are incredibly rare and valuable. Here are some of the most famous meteorites and tektites known to us:

- **Allende Meteorite:** The Allende meteorite is the largest carbonaceous chondrite ever found, weighing over two tons. It was first discovered in 1969 in the Chihuahuan Desert of northern Mexico. This meteorite is fascinating because it contains pre-solar grains, which are grains of stardust that predate our Solar System. These grains give insight into the universe's conditions before the formation of our own Solar System.
- **Fukang Meteorite:** The Fukang meteorite was discovered in 2000 in the Gobi Desert in China. It's a type of pallasite meteorite, which means it is made up of iron-nickel and silicate materials. This meteorite is unique because it contains some of the largest olivine crystals ever found, some up to 10 centimeters across. It's also one of the most visually stunning meteorites, with a beautiful green and yellow coloration.
- **Esquel Meteorite:** The Esquel meteorite was discovered in 1951 in Argentina and is one of the few meteorites composed entirely of nickel-iron metal. It's also a fantastic example of a meteorite's Widmanstätten pattern, which is a unique crystalline structure that forms due to the slow cooling of an iron-nickel alloy. The pattern is a visually stunning reminder of the meteorite's journey through space.
- **Moldavite Tektite:** Moldavite is a glassy green rock that is thought to have formed around 15 million years ago when a meteorite hit the Earth. It's found mainly in the Czech Republic and is one of the most valuable tektites in the world. What makes moldavite so fascinating is its unique composition, which contains rare elements not found on Earth. It's also believed to have mystical properties and is valued by collectors and spiritualists.
- **Libyan Glass Tektite:** The Libyan glass tektite is a type of tektite that formed around 26 million years ago when a meteorite hit the Earth in what is now Western Egypt. It's a rare and valuable specimen due to its unique composition and the fact that it's believed to contain evidence of water on the moon. It's also

been found to contain high levels of helium-three, a rare isotope that's highly valuable for scientific research.
- **Darwin Glass Tektite:** The Darwin glass tektite is a type of tektite found in Tasmania, Australia. It's named after Charles Darwin, who first discovered the glassy rock in 1838 during his voyage on HMS Beagle. This tektite is fascinating because it is believed to have formed from a meteorite impact over 800,000 years ago. It is also one of the most visually stunning tektites, with a deep green color and natural bubble patterns that make it highly sought after by collectors.

Ways to Identify and Test a Meteorite

1. **Shape:** One of the easiest ways to identify a meteorite is by its shape. Meteorites are typically very irregular in shape and often have a pitted or grooved surface. If you find a rock that has a smooth, rounded shape, it is likely not a meteorite.
2. **Color:** Another way to identify a meteorite is by its color. Meteorites are often darker in color than other rocks due to their high iron content. If you find a rock that is very light in color, it is likely not a meteorite.
3. **Weight:** Meteorites are also much heavier than other rocks due to their high density. If you find a rock that is very light in weight, it is likely not a meteorite.
4. **Magnetism:** One way to test if a rock is a meteorite is by using a magnet. Meteorites are attracted to magnets due to their high iron content. If the rock you are testing is not attracted to a magnet, it is likely not a meteorite.
5. **Acid Test:** Another way to test if a rock is a meteorite is by using acid. Meteorites contain high levels of iron, which will react with acid. If the rock you are testing does not react with acid, it is likely not a meteorite.

Meteorites and tektites are fascinating remnants of our solar system's past. These rocks are valuable not just for their scientific value but also for their aesthetic beauty. Meteorites provide insight into the formation of our planets, and tektites provide clues about ancient impacts on the Earth. By studying meteorites and tektites, we can learn more about our solar system's history and better understand the amazing forces that shaped it. From the visually stunning Widmanstätten pattern to the mystical properties of moldavite, these rocks offer a window into our universe's past.

Appendix: A-Z of Rocks, Crystals, Gems, and Minerals

Now that you have familiarized yourself with the basics of rocks, crystals, gems, and minerals, let's dive a little deeper. Below is an alphabetical list of various types with quick reference details:

Amber - A fossilized tree resin that is often found in the form of a gemstone. It can be between 30 and 90 million years old.

Agate - A variety of chalcedony with various patterns and colors, often formed in cavities of other rocks.

Amethyst - A type of quartz, often purple, used to make jewelry and other decorative objects.

Apatite - A phosphorous mineral that is the main component of teeth and bones.

Azurite - A copper mineral that ranges in color from deep blue to green.

Beryl - A family of minerals that includes emeralds and aquamarine.

Chalcedony - A form of quartz that is found in a variety of colors.

Diamond - A hard, clear mineral that is the hardest natural substance known.

Fluorite - A mineral composed of calcium and fluorine atoms with a variety of colors.

Garnet - A group of minerals that come in a range of colors and are used in jewelry.

Hematite – A mineral that is often black or steel-gray and used as a pigment in paint.

Jade – An ornamental stone, usually green, used for centuries to make jewelry and sculptures.

Kyanite – A blue or green mineral that is often used as a gemstone.

Labradorite – A mineral with an iridescent quality, typically gray.

Lapis Lazuli – A rock composed of several minerals, including lazurite, pyrite, and calcite.

Malachite – A green mineral that is often found in the upper layers of copper-bearing ores.

Opal – A type of mineraloid composed of silica and water molecules with a variety of colors and iridescent qualities.

Quartz – A mineral composed of silicon and oxygen atoms with a variety of forms and colors.

Sapphire – Corundum in its purest form, typically blue, but can be found in other colors.

Tiger's Eye – A chatoyant gemstone often used for jewelry and ornamentation.

Topaz – A mineral that comes in many colors, including yellow and blue.

Turquoise – An opaque, green-blue mineral often used for jewelry and ornamentation.

Zircon – A hard, durable mineral with a variety of colors, such as yellow and red.

We hope this list has provided useful reference information about the various types of rocks, crystals, gems, and minerals available. Happy collecting!

Conclusion

Rocks, gems, and minerals are intricate geological features that have captivated the imagination of humans for centuries. We marvel at their stunning beauty, exquisite texture, and complex composition. They provide us with an endless source of entertainment while also informally educating us on the processes of creation and erosion. There is something special about standing in awe of a beautiful landscape or precious stone. All these geologic wonders unveil secrets of our natural world to those curious enough to find them.

Geology is an endlessly fascinating science with a world of natural wonders that never fails to amaze. Whether it's the seemingly infinite varieties of rocks, or the bright and dazzling gems and minerals, each is a unique specimen that requires thousands of years to form and create. A single rock can tell you a multitude of stories about its journey. Every crystal and gem has an almost magical beauty. It's no surprise that they have been credited with ancient powers since time immemorial. Taking the time to explore geology is sure to provide you with an educational experience like no other.

From the basics of why each is important to uncovering unique and precious stones from different parts of the world, no stone has gone unturned. We take an exciting journey through each geological process that leads us to discoveries for different types of rocks, including igneous, sedimentary, and metamorphic. Whether it be research or simply gathering knowledge out of curiosity, this guide provides a comprehensive path to understanding more about our Earth's wonders with its valuable content.

This book is a treasure trove of knowledge, giving readers an in-depth look into the fascinating world of crystal systems and quartz formations. With this resource, we've learned about both precious and semi-precious gemstones and discovered the mysterious buried secrets tektites and meteorites keep. Lastly, the helpful A-Z guide at the end of this book makes it easy to identify which rocks are valuable minerals and which aren't.

Exploring the natural world can be a great way to find rocks, gems, crystals, and minerals that can all serve as special treasures. Whether hiking in the woods or rummaging through your local farmers market, you never know what you might find. Rocks and gemstones have been prized for centuries as sources of beauty and power. Crystals are also said to have healing properties and can serve as powerful energizers when placed in specific areas of your living space. Lastly, minerals can often be found in everyday elements unusually rich in certain metals or other elements. Have fun exploring the crystal realms and see what magical discoveries you might stumble upon!

Here's another book by Mari Silva that you might like

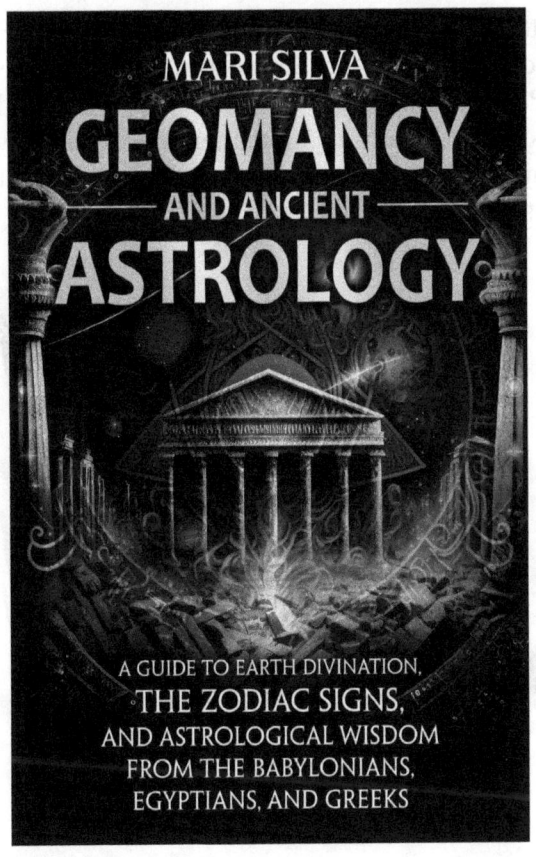

Your Free Gift
(only available for a limited time)

Thanks for getting this book! If you want to learn more about various spirituality topics, then join Mari Silva's community and get a free guided meditation MP3 for awakening your third eye. This guided meditation mp3 is designed to open and strengthen ones third eye so you can experience a higher state of consciousness. Simply visit the link below the image to get started.

https://spiritualityspot.com/meditation

References

(N.d.). Thekidshouldseethis.com. https://thekidshouldseethis.com/post/gems-minerals-crystals-and-rocks-whats-the-difference

Farndon, J. (2017). Rocks, Minerals, and Gems. Australian Geographic.

Gem & mineral identification. (n.d.). Treasure Quest Mining. https://treasurequestmining.com/treasure-identification/gems/

Identifying minerals. (n.d.). Google Arts & Culture. https://artsandculture.google.com/story/QgXh9pyyxhIYKQ

King, H. M. (n.d.). Gemstones. Geology.com. https://geology.com/gemstones/

List of gemstones: Precious and semi-precious stones - gem society. (2016, June 8). International Gem Society; International Gem Society LLC. https://www.gemsociety.org/gemstone-encyclopedia/

Minerals and gems. (2017, January 15). National Geographic. https://www.nationalgeographic.com/science/article/minerals-gems

Somarin, A. (2014, March 20). Where did those gemstones come from? Advancing Mining. https://www.thermofisher.com/blog/mining/where-did-those-gemstones-come-from/

Using characteristics of minerals to identify them. (n.d.). Illinois.edu. https://isgs.illinois.edu/outreach/geology-resources/using-characteristics-minerals-identify-them

www.ingramcontent.com/pod-product-compliance
Lightning Source LLC
Chambersburg PA
CBHW051847160426
43209CB00006B/1194